Amazon Echo Show

The Complete User Guide:
Learn to Use Your Echo Show Like A Pro

by C.J. Andersen

AMAZON ECHO SHOW

THE COMPLETE USER GUIDE : LEARN TO USE YOUR ECHO SHOW LIKE A PRO

LATEST EDITION 2017

C.J. ANDERSEN

Alexa Enabled Amazon Devices

Echo Show

Echo

Echo Dot

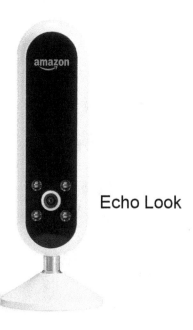

Echo Look

Fire Tablets

Fire Stick

Contents

Introduction

Hello and welcome! Thank you for buying this Echo Show user guide and I look forward to sharing my knowledge and helping you to master your new Amazon device. Before we get under way I would like to make a couple of suggestions. Firstly, I would like to encourage you to sign up to my monthly Alexa Updates Newsletter and here's why... Amazon is constantly tweaking, updating and expanding the capabilities of both its devices (Fire tablets, Fire TV, Echo, Echo Dot, Echo Show etc) and its AI software Alexa.

And when I say constantly I mean ALL the time.

The Echo Show has only been available for a few months and there have already been a number of improvements and noteworthy additions in the time it has taken me to write this guide. While I will continue to publish updated editions of this guide I want to be sure that anyone who has bought this book has the chance to stay up to date with the frequent changes. My Alexa Updates Newsletter is the solution. Once a month I will send out a roundup of any significant or newsworthy developments that will enhance the use of your Alexa enabled Amazon device...including the Echo Show.

Of course you can unsubscribe from the newsletter at any time and I will *never* share your personal information with anyone. So go ahead and **Subscribe Today** at www.about.me/cjandersen.

Secondly, I wanted to say a word about this guide, how it has been put together and the best way to use it. Of course, you should feel free to dip into a particular chapter if there is some specific information you are looking for, but I would also urge you to read the book from start to finish as it follows a logical progression. If this is your first Alexa enabled Amazon device then you will discover that the Alexa app is at the heart of everything you can do with the Echo Show. For that reason I have laid out this guide to take you step by step through every option within the app starting at the top and working down to the bottom. It's really the easiest way to approach and master Alexa without jumping back and forth and getting lost in the numerous options.

I am confident that anyone, no matter what level their tech skills, will find learning and using their Amazon Echo Show pretty straight forward. If there's anything that you still find confusing after having read this guide then please email me at cjandersentech@gmail.com

Okay, let's go!

Before the Show Starts: Echo Show Basics

As an enthusiastic user of the Amazon Echo, I was eager for the Show to makes its appearance and have been very happy with its performance.

The original Echo now sits in my bedroom where it answers questions about the time, my commute or the temperature outside, sets alarms, plays instrumental music while I'm reading in bed or news and weather in the morning when I'm getting ready for the day. Though the Echo Show can do all those things, I prefer to place it where I can make use of its visual capabilities.

The Show has taken Echo's old place on the breakfast bar in the kitchen where I can:

- Look at the weather forecast

- Watch a video while eating breakfast

- Shop on Amazon

- Read or listen to a recipe when cooking

- Make use of all the other visual and non-visual benefits this personal assistant offers

One of the things I like best is that most of the information requested from Echo Show also shows up on the Alexa App (more later), so I can view it there immediately or later when I want to review it.

If I unplug and move the Echo Show, the device takes just a minute or two to reboot and connect to Wi-Fi.

A quick note on the wake word: Echo Show requires a wake word to activate your device. For example, "Alexa, what's the weather like today" where "Alexa" is your wake word. I'm guessing you already know that, so in this guide I don't include a wake word when suggesting what to say to Alexa. For any voice command you read in this guide be sure to use your wake word first.

The Echo Show Preview

Getting started with Echo Show takes just a few minutes, and most of the setup happens automatically. Before you plug it in, though, look over the Show to familiarize yourself with the physical features of the hardware and the purpose of each.

On/Off, Mic & Camera Button: There are three buttons on the top of the device. This information is about the left button as the screen faces you:

- **On:** To turn on the device, press and hold the button for about three seconds. The "Amazon" logo will appear shortly to let you know the device is on.

- **Disable Mic and Camera:** Press and quickly release this button to turn off the mic and camera. A small red light will appear above the screen and the light bar will turn red to indicate the mic and camera are disabled, and Alexa won't "hear" the wake word. When these functions are disabled, you'll only be able to communicate with the device using the Alexa Voice Remote, a handy tool that is sold separately and discussed in the next chapter. Your primary reason for disabling the mic is to communicate with Alexa through the remote, for example if you're across the room and there are other conversations going on that might confuse the device if it were picking up everything being said. Note: There are eight microphones distributed beneath the oval of holes surrounding the top buttons. This assists the device in picking up your voice from anywhere in the room.

- **Off:** To turn off Echo Show, press the button and hold slightly longer. The "Power off" option will appear with the question, "Are you sure you want to shut down your device?" Touch "cancel" or "OK" to confirm your choice.

Volume Buttons: The middle button (-) turns the volume down; the right button (+) turns it up. The level shows on the screen as you push the buttons, and the device will beep to let you know what volume you've selected.

Camera: The camera is in front, above the screen. It's a 5MP camera that takes excellent pictures.

Touch Screen: The 7" color touch screen can be used for many Echo Show functions including shopping, browsing entertainment or checking out the suggestions Alexa rotates on the screen.

Light bar: The LED light bar extends across the bottom of the screen and gives a variety of indications:

- **Blue and green intermingled:** Alexa is listening.
- **Blue:** Alexa is processing your request.
- **Red:** Mic/camera are disabled.
- **Orange:** Echo Show is having Wi-Fi connectivity issues (See Troubleshooting for details on trouble connecting to Wi-Fi).
- **Purple:** "Do Not Disturb" is on; A crescent moon also appears on the screen. This feature is explained below.
- **No lights:** If Echo Show is on and the light bar is off, the device is ready and waiting.

Power supply and port: The power supply plugs into the back of the device near the bottom.

This Amazon page (https://amzn.to/2uKSFwl) covers the same information and can serve as a handy reference.

Specifications of the Amazon Echo Show

In case you're wondering, here are the specs of the device in front of you.

Dimensions and Weight:

- Height: 7.375 inches
- Width: 7.375 inches
- Base depth: 3.625"
- Weight: 42.3 ounces

Screen: 7" diagonal

Processor: Intel Atom

Networking:

- Wireless
- 802.11a/b/g/n, Bluetooth wireless protocol

- Dual-band (2.4 GHz and 5 GHz)
- Bluetooth, IEEE 802.11a IEEE 802.11b, IEEE 802.11g, IEEE 802.11n data link protocol
- For security reasons, Echo Show does not connect to ad-hoc or peer-to-peer networks

Warranty: 1 year

Current Echo Show Hardware Accessories:

- Covers of various materials with handles
- Tempered glass screen protectors
- Acrylic stand
- Wall-mounted shelf
- Third-party protection plans for 1, 2, and 3 years

You can visit https://amzn.to/2uKEIii for Amazon approved accessories or here https://amzn.to/2i9kN6q for third party offers.

I bought two accessories for my Echo Show:

- A tempered glass screen protector for $12 since I recently had a Samsung tablet screen crack, and the repair cost exceeded $125 (the protector does not diminish touch screen functionality)
- A clear acrylic shelf for $18 that keeps Echo Show slightly off the countertop, out of the path of spilled water and other hazards

Echo Vs Echo Show

Perhaps you're wondering whether the Echo Show was the right purchase or if you'd have been just as happy with the standard Echo. I've got both, enjoy both, and if I had to choose one or the other, I'd take the Echo Show for the visual aspect. They each have pros and cons, however.

The Echo and Echo Show have much in common including that neither are portable, both run off a plug-in power adapter and they have the same Wi-Fi protocol and data link protocol.

Both have these capabilities:

- Bluetooth audio input
- Bluetooth audio output
- Compatibility with Alexa Voice Remote
- Broad personal assistant capabilities through Alexa (Lists, timers, alarms, reminders, calendars, notifications, etc.)
- Media services like Amazon Music, Spotify and iHeartRadio

Neither device has:

- AUX audio input or output
- Media storage
- The Alexa Voice Remote included

Now, here's how Echo Show is different than Echo:

- Echo Show has a 7" color screen
- Echo has one speaker (mono); Echo Show has two (stereo)
- Echo Show has Dolby audio

The screen is what sets the Echo Show apart, of course, and I have found the screen to be a definite plus when seeing is better than hearing: Shopping on Amazon, viewing the weather forecast at a glance or reviewing my To-do list.

Note on the Echo Show sound: With two speakers and Dolby, you'd expect the sound on the Echo Show to be superior than on the Echo, and I think it is – but only at low and mid-range volume. I suspect the speaker quality is fairly average although I haven't dismantled the device to examine them. Perhaps cutting cost on speakers is a necessary step in keeping the Show's price where it is while including outstanding screen quality. The Echo's single speaker is more robust and handles higher volume better. The Echo Show speakers can get a little buzzy. That's my opinion, for what it's worth.

1: Let the Show Begin! — Echo Show Setup

For any voice command you read in this chapter be sure to use your wake word ("Alexa", "Amazon", etc) first.

Setting up Echo Show is largely an automated process once you plug in the device. Here's what should have come in the box:

- Echo Show
- Power adapter with 6' cord
- Echo Show startup tri-fold guide
- Echo Show "Things to Try" card

The pieces of protective film over the screen and speaker can be removed by pulling the blue tabs.

Echo Show Placement: My Show has a semi-permanent spot on the breakfast bar. Perhaps try several locations to determine where you get maximum usage from your Echo Show, and, if you're like me, you will move it occasionally.

Wherever you place the device, Amazon recommends it be at least eight inches from walls and windows, so that indoor echoes and outdoor noises don't confuse poor Alexa!

Starting the Echo Show: OK, enough with the preliminaries. Let's get the Show going. Have your Wi-Fi password and your Amazon login information available for connection and setup.

1: Download the Alexa app to your phone and/or tablet (or see 5: below if you don't have a mobile device)

Mobile device requirements are:

- FireOS 3.0 or higher
- Android 5.0 or higher
- iOS 9.0 or higher

The quickest method for downloading the app is to go to the app store on your mobile device, look up the Alexa app and install it.

Accessing the App and Settings: Once the Alexa App is installed, you will be able to access it on your mobile device and at alexa.amazon. com on your PC or Mac. It's a good idea to locate Settings on the App, because they are referred to often. You can also access an abbreviated list of settings on the Echo device. To do this, place two fingers (Amazon's recommendation) on the glass above the screen, to the right of the camera, for example. I prefer using my thumb, and it works just as well. Slide your fingers down, and a toolbar will appear with:

- Home – the Default screen that you can customize in the Settings
- Settings
- The Do Not Disturb button and its status
- The brightness adjuster

2: Plug in/Turn on Echo Show

Plug the adapter into Echo Show and an outlet, and the device will turn on.

3: Follow the Prompts

The prompts walk you through:

- Selecting a language
- Connecting to the Wi-Fi network you select from a list of those available
- Logging into your Amazon account
- Reviewing Echo Show Terms and Conditions

If your network isn't in the list, you can add it or view the Advanced Wi-Fi options by scrolling to the bottom of the page. You can also connect to Wi-Fi using Settings on the Echo Show:

- Slide the screen down to show the toolbar

- Tap **Settings** > Tap **Wi-Fi**

- View Available Networks, and tap the network you want to connect to and enter your network password

- If you prefer, tap **Add a Network**

- Manually enter the SSID, or tap the microphone in the middle of the screen and speak the SSID when the microphone turns blue

- Select **Done** to complete adding a network

Connection trouble: If your Echo Show does not connect to Wi-Fi, its light bar will be orange. Try these troubleshooting and solution tips in this order:

- Make sure your Wi-Fi is on

- Use another Wi-Fi device such as a tablet or computer to ensure Wi-Fi is working

- Tap the network you want to connect to and select the **Forget** option to reset the connection

- Attempt to connect to the network

- Make sure your network password (different than your Amazon password) is correct, and retry it

- If you saved your Wi-Fi password to Amazon but later changed it, you'll need to update the information on Amazon

- Turn off other devices connected to Wi-Fi; they might be causing too much congestion on the network for the Echo Show to connect

- Move your Echo Show away from a baby monitor or microwave oven that might be causing interference

- Try to connect to your router's 5GHz Wi-Fi frequency, if one is available, since that band might be less congested

Intermittent Wi-Fi: Sometimes an interruption in Wi-Fi prevents a connection. If your Wi-Fi goes out for brief periods, try this:

- Turn off the network hardware (router and separate modem if there is one)

- Wait 20-30 seconds

- Turn the modem on

- Turn the router on, if separate

- Unplug the Echo Show device, and plug it in again after three seconds

- Attempt the connection to Wi-Fi again

If nothing works, contact your Internet provider or router manufacturer. If your network has an administrator, they might be able to help too.

4: Pair mobile devices with Echo Show

I recommend taking this step now since you're in a Startup frame of mind. This is a separate function from downloading the App to your device and using Echo Show from there. Since Echo Show is Bluetooth-enabled, you can use it as a standalone Bluetooth speaker to stream your favorite audio services from your tablet or phone. This is important for users who predominately use Google Play Music and iTunes on their mobiles.

- Go to your phone's or other device's Settings and select Bluetooth to ensure that Bluetooth is On

- Say, "Pair my phone" or "pair my tablet," or go to Settings on the Echo device, tap Bluetooth, and pairing will occur

- Alexa will say, "Connected to _____ phone"

- The Bluetooth Setting on the screen will list Bluetooth devices paired and whether they are connected

- Your device's Bluetooth Settings should list your Echo Show when the two are paired

- Say, "Cancel," to stop Bluetooth pairing if you want to exit the mode before connection

- **Note**: If you have paired Echo Show with several mobile devices, it will connect to the most recently paired device. You can only pair with one device at a time.

- To disconnect a device that is paired, say, "Disconnect"

5: Access the Alexa App on your computer, and sign in (optional)

This is my preferred way to use the app, followed by using my tablet and finally the phone. I like the larger view. The App address is: <u>alexa.amazon.com</u>

6: Customize the Echo Show device home screen and Sounds

I suggest you wait a few days or a week before customizing the device home screen to see how you like default mode, but the information is included here as part of the general setup process.

- Go to **Settings** on the device, you can use the touch screen with your fingers as described above or say "Go to Settings"

- Tap **Home Screen**

- Tap **Background** to change the background from Default to a photo uploaded from your phone via the Alexa App or one from your Prime Photos collection, which is explained in Chapter 13 (page 105)

- Use the Back arrow to go back to the Home Screen settings, and tap **Home Card Preferences** to choose whether things like Notifications, Upcoming Events and Trending Topics (all explained shortly) appear on your screen and how often they appear

- From the **Settings** page, tap **Display** to customize the screen more comprehensively with easy-to-follow prompts

- For choosing sounds preferences, go to the device's **Settings**, tap **Sounds** and choose levels for Media volume and Alarm, Timer and Notification Volume before browsing Custom Sounds (Alarm sounds are discussed in Chapter 8 (page 63)

I turned off the Trending Topics from the home screen within a couple of hours. To me, they were like squirrels running past the window, causing me to turn to look at them every time a new one appeared. If they distract you too:

- Go to **Settings** on the Echo Show

- Tap **Home Screen** > tap **Home Card Preferences** > Scroll to the bottom of the page > Tap the **Trending Topics** button to turn them off, and the blue dot will turn white and move from the right to left of the oval

There are two other solutions when Echo Show's screen is distracting you — turn it away from you or say, "Turn off your screen." With the voice command, the screen will go dark until you tap it or make a new request.

7: Create an Amazon Household

This is another setup feature you might want to wait till later to do, if at all.

If there are other Amazonians in your household — your literal or figurative "household" — you might want to share capabilities such as being able to listen to each other's music. Explore the benefits and how-to's of Amazon Households by following the instructions below or going to https://www.amazon.com/myh/manage.

- On Amazon.com hover over **Accounts & Lists** near the top of the page

- Select "Your Account"

- In the "Shopping programs and rentals" box (bottom right), select **Amazon Households** to go to the Manage Your Household / Your Amazon Household Benefits page

- Select "Add an Adult," and follow the instructions including providing their login information, so they will have to give it to you or be there with you to type it in

- And/or select "Add a Child," Create and Save their Profile, and follow the link to Manage Your Content and Devices to determine the content they can access

8: Set up the Alexa voice remote (optional)

The Alexa voice remote is available on Amazon for $29.99 (www.amzn. to/2v4e9Q8). Its availability has been intermittent, though at this writing, it is in stock. Be aware that there is also an Alexa voice remote for Amazon Fire TV and Fire TV Stick. That's not what you want here. While Echo Show is equipped with Far-field voice recognition to pick up the wake word and queries, there are times the remote is a handy alternative to talking across the room, especially when there is other noise in the space that will cause you to shout or that will confuse Alexa.

If you want a preview of Echo Show's shopping abilities, say, "Shop for Alexa voice remote," and watch your screen! Beware that if 1-Click is turned on in your Amazon account and you select **Buy This** on the screen, you will indeed make a purchase. Immediately saying, "Cancel the order" will reverse it.

Once the remote's batteries are installed, it might pair automatically. This has been hit and miss with users. If it doesn't, you can pair it via the Alexa App or on the Echo Show device.

Pair the remote using the app:

- Go to *Settings*
- Select your device (your Echo Show)
- Select *Pair Remote*

Pair the remote using the device:

- Swipe down from the top of the touch screen
- Choose *Settings*
- Scroll down the page by gently swiping up on the screen
- Choose *Device Options*
- Scroll down the Device Options page to *Pair Amazon Echo Remote*
- Follow the brief directions given there

2: Meet the Show's Director — The Alexa App

For any voice command you read in this chapter be sure to use your wake word ("Alexa", "Amazon", etc) first.

Now that Setup is complete, you'll get the most utility from Echo Show and complete tasks more quickly if you know your way around the Alexa App. We will refer to Settings several times here. They are a part of the App, but there's so much information to share about Settings that it has its own chapter (page 89). It's inevitable that some information will be covered in both places.

Amazon calls Alexa the "brain behind the Amazon Echo Show" and other Echo devices. Alexa is cloud-based, making it possible for Alexa and Echo Show to continually be improved and updated. If you're worried about security, consider that it's likely that many of your accounts are already somewhere in the cloud — banking, credit cards, medical in addition to other Amazon accounts such as Prime or Drive. The same level of security used with that information is used with Alexa.

The App, your Voice and the Screen

Most of what you can do via the Alexa App can also be done with voice. If you're listening to an Amazon music station, for example, you can select the Pause button on the app or simply say, "pause." In the remainder of this guide, we will note things you cannot do by voice, such as Change the Wake Word. In all other cases, assume you can accomplish the task with your voice, and give it a try.

There is also interplay between the App and the touch screen. For example, when you're listening to media, the Now Playing page will display on the Echo Show screen, and when you add an item to your Shopping List, the list will appear for about 30 seconds before the screen reverts to its Default display. The display can be customized in **Settings** on the App and on the Echo Show device.

Note on clarifying terms: In tech talk about devices, the terms "page" and "screen" are sometimes used interchangeably in a confusing manner. To be clear, in this guide, a "page" is a page on the app you can view on your phone, tablet or computer; the "screen" is the Echo Show device touch screen.

A Word about Help & Feedback

The **Help & Feedback** page, accessible within the Alexa app, is discussed in detail later, but it's worth knowing before we get started that this section contains a wealth of information about all the topics discussed throughout the rest of this book.

Alexa App Home Page

As you view the app layout at Alexa.Amazon.com, you'll see a Menu of app pages on the left and the current page on the right. That's what you might see on large mobile devices too, but on most phones and tablets, you will see just the current page. The Menu will be depicted with three horizontal lines.

Now, let's explore the Home page, starting at the top. It includes Things to Try, your Cards and, when you're playing most media, a music player.

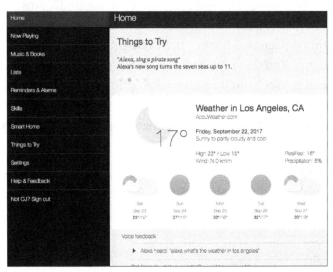

Things to Try: When on the Home page, a Things to Try feature appears at the top. It rotates through some suggestions of things to say to Alexa related to current or trending issues.

There are shaded buttons below the suggestions. I click or tap manually through them since I don't have the patience to watch them rotate at the rate of 7–8 seconds per suggestion. Occasionally something of interest appears, like Sports Jeopardy — Put your sports smarts to the test — but I've found they can be a time waster in the same way social media can be when there are other things I should be doing.

Cards: A Card is created with most verbal interactions with Alexa. The Card preserves the request and response from Alexa such as music station or a forecast you requested, a recipe you've selected, a Skill used or items you added to your shopping list.

Cards form your Alexa Dialog History. You can scroll down the Cards to review them. A list of them is also available in Settings. Select **Settings**, and scroll down to the General section, and select **History**.

Card options: The top Card in your history will show options for further action:

- **Remove card:** Select this to delete the card

- **Give Voice feedback:** The Card will show what "Alex heard" with the question, "Did Alexa do what you wanted?" Answering the question helps Alexa improve its understanding of how you speak, something discussed further in **Settings > Accounts > Voice Training**. You don't have to answer the question, of course. If you answer "no," you'll be given the option to "Send more detailed feedback. Select that for unlimited space to provide feedback and the opportunity to request that Amazon get back to you on your input.

- **Learn More:** This takes you to Alexa and Alexa Device FAQs, which is a useful part of the Help & Feedback section of the Menu I recommend you browse when you have a few minutes.

To use these options on older Cards, select ***More***, and the box will expand to show them.

Deleting your entire history at once is only possible by deregistering your device, something you'd likely do only if giving it away or selling it. Deregistering Echo Show and reregistering it is explained in the Settings section.

Bing Search and Wikipedia: One or both these options might appear on a Card:

- **Search Bing:** If Alexa is unclear about what you say or if you ask about a person, place or thing, Alexa will provide the option to "Search Bing for..." whatever your query was about. Bing is your only search engine option on the App.

- **Learn more on Wikipedia:** Depending on the subject you ask Alexa about, the Card might give you a short answer and a link to the topic on Wikipedia.

Player: When media is loaded, whether playing or paused, the Player at the bottom of the Home page allows you to control it. The bar includes an icon of the current song in the queue. The Player appears at the bottom of the App regardless of what page you're on. It is discussed fully in the Now Playing section next.

3: What's Show-ing? — The 'Now Playing' Homepage and Player

For any voice command you read in this chapter be sure to use your wake word ("Alexa", "Amazon", etc) first.

One of Alexa's most attractive features is its ability to play media from a wide range of sources. Those platforms are explored in detail in the next chapter: **Music, Videos & Books**. There, we'll also discuss how to make a request for specific music or a general request such as, "Play Acoustic Indie music." For many of the media, the Now Playing page displays an icon for the source such as iHeartRadio, Kindle audiobooks or a podcast on Tunein to remind you where the media is coming from.

You can manually tap or click any option on the Now Playing page or you can use voice.

The player always offers these control symbols:

- **Play/Pause:** Manually select or say, "Pause," "Resume," "Play" or "Stop."

- **Go back:** Manually select or say, "Go back."

- **Go forward:** Manually select or say, "Go forward."

- **Sound level vertical slide:** Slide the volume bar manually by "grabbing" it or use a verbal command such as "volume seven" or "mute."

- **Song progress bar:** When using the App on a computer, selecting a place earlier or later in the song isn't possible. Ability to change the place in the song varies on mobile devices. Another option is to use the touch screen to drag the song location back or forth.

When playing music from an Amazon station, playlist or other collection, additional options are shown on the player:

- **Thumb Up & Thumb Down:** Rate the song, and Alexa will use your opinion to tailor your music stations to your preferences

- **Shuffle:** Selecting the crossed arrows will cause the Queue to be played in random order

- **Repeat:** Select the looping arrows to repeat the song or station when it is completed

In the upper right of the Now Playing page are two lists you can view Queue and History by selecting your choice.

Queue: This is the list of selections in the media you've chosen such as the Classical Focus Prime Station I'm currently enjoying. Expand your options for each piece by selecting the V-shaped symbol known as a caret. For music, expanding the box allows you to:

- Rate the song by choosing Thumb Up or Thumb Down

- Shop the Digital Music Store, which will open in a new page with the standard features seen on all Amazon product pages

- View album in Prime Music, if applicable, which will open in a page that looks very much like the Digital Store page but with the opportunity to buy any/all the songs on the recording

- When listening to podcasts or radio stations, clicking the caret and expanding the box allows you to mark what your listening to as a *Favorite program*

History: This is the list of media you've played from all sources.

Note that if you are playing a station and then select another media, the station might be canceled. I learned this by pausing a station and asking for my news Flash Briefing, explained later but found in *Settings* if you want to explore it before we get to it. The station did not resume, even at my request. Stations are not canceled if you ask for your Forecast, something from Wikipedia or a simple question. The station volume is reduced while Alexa fulfills the request. I'm still learning which requests cancel stations and which don't. If a station gets canceled, and I want to continue listening, it's right there in History where I can pick up where I left off.

Play anything from Queue or History by tapping/clicking it. Your choice will then become the Now Playing media.

Now Playing on the Echo Show Screen

Most media will appear on the Echo Show screen too, but the Player control options might be more limited. Tap the screen to see the player, and tap the appropriate control to pause, play, go back or forward one song, drag the song to the end, shuffle the songs or repeat.

4: Watch This and More!
— Video

For any voice command you read in this chapter be sure to use your wake word ("Alexa", "Amazon", etc) first.

This is the first section listed in the App's Music, Video & Books section, so that's where we will begin. The section's title covers a lot of ground and still doesn't fully capture all that's available here. Video is new to the Echo universe with the introduction of the Echo Show. Music continues to grow, and the Books platforms, Kindle for eBooks (Amazon simply refers to them as Books now) and Audible for audiobooks, have their enthusiastic users too.

Let's take the list of services on this page from top to bottom. Since Amazon continues to update what's available, the list might change, as it did while writing this book, and be different when you're reading it. The good news is that each service sets up very easily.

The basic idea for all the services is that you establish an account with the service and then link Alexa/Echo Show to it.

At this writing, Alexa Video supports Fire TV and Dish TV, though Amazon reports it is "working hard to bring additional services to Alexa."

Watch Amazon Video on Echo Show

Amazon Video is a huge offering of digital movies and TV shows you can watch on Echo Show by simply asking for a title. The media can also be watched on computers, Amazon Fire devices, iOS and Android devices, TVs and more. Let's talk about Amazon Video on Echo Show.

Video can be obtained from three sources:

- **Amazon Video:** Digital versions of movies, TV shows and series and any other video content that you've purchased individually from Amazon to form your Video Library.

- **Amazon Prime Membership and Prime for Students:** Thousands of video titles for movies, TV shows and Amazon original content are available at no additional cost with a Prime trial or membership. To see what's on offer go to the Amazon Video department on the Amazon website and click the tab that says Included with Prime

- **Video Subscriptions:** Hundreds of premium third-party channels like HBO, Starz and Showtime plus many for kids and other niche genres are not free with Prime but can be subscribed to individually from the Amazon website. To see these third party services again go to the Amazon Video page and this time click the Channels tab

Join Amazon Prime by selecting Try Prime near the top left of any Amazon page.

Watch Video on Echo Show: Once you've got something to watch, there are many ways you can access it.

- **Search your library:** Say "Show me my video library" or "Show me my watchlist," and it will appear on the Show screen where you can browse by swiping left and tapping what you want to watch.

- **Search by title:** Say "Show me [specific movie or show title], and it will play

- **Show by actor or genre:** Say, "Show me Harrison Ford movies," or "Show me animated movies," and search results you can browse will appear on the Echo Show screen.

Alexa will reply, "Here's what I found," to all these requests as the results appear.

Once the content is being shown, you can control it two ways:

- Tap the Echo Show screen to view and use the limited player that includes pause/play and symbols for going back or forward 10 seconds

- Use voice with common commands including:

— Play/pause/resume

— Rewind/fast forward

— Go back/skip ahead and number of seconds, minutes or hours

— Next video/next episode

Tapping the screen will produce a back arrow that can be used to go back to the last content played or to the search results.

Watch Movie Trailers on Echo Show

You can watch any move trailer from IMDB on Echo Show by simply asking. Say, "Show me the movie trailer for [movie title]."

You can control the trailer playback two ways:

• Tap the Echo Show screen to view and use the limited player that includes pause/play and symbols for going back or forward 10 seconds

• Use voice with common commands including:

— Play/pause/resume

— Rewind/fast forward

— Go back/skip ahead and number of seconds

I really like using my Echo Show to watch movie trailers, they are exactly the kind of short video content that work really well on the small Echo Show screen. I'm not convinced there's much value in being able to play the rest of my Amazon Video Library on the Show. I've watched a couple of half hour TV shows, but I won't watch anything longer as I'd far prefer to view most TV series and movies on a bigger screen like my TV. In fact that brings us neatly to Amazon's Fire TV. Using the Alexa to operate your Fire TV is definitely useful!

Fire TV

This Amazon product line is a comprehensive media and personal assistant center that can be paired with and controlled by an Echo device. So to be clear, if you would like to use Fire TV with your Echo Show you will need to buy one of the Fire TV device options.

What you can watch with Fire TV: Most streaming and live TV services can be viewed with Fire TV including: Netflix, Hulu, HBO Now, Crackle, Amazon, ESPN, Showtime, Sling, DirectTV Now, NBA, MLB. TV, CNN, Comedy Central, HGTV and AMC.

What else you can do with Fire TV and Alexa: Enjoy music services played through your equipment such as Amazon Music, and iHeartRadio, order pizza or an Uber, browse Yelp and play games from developers like EA and Disney. Search "Fire TV" on Amazon to see everything the service offers.

Connecting Alexa and Fire TV: Amazon provides complete instructions for setting up Fire TV equipment and a PDF Users Guide to make the most of Fire TV. To control Fire TV with Alexa:

- Go to *Music, Video & Books* in the Alexa App, and select *Fire TV*
- Select *Link Your Alexa Device*
- Select the device you want to link
- Follow the onscreen prompts to complete linking of Alexa to the Fire TV Player

Once setup is complete, put Alexa to work with requests like:

- "Watch House of Cards"
- "Next episode"
- "Rewind 10 minutes"
- "Jump to 30 minutes"
- "Show me Emma Watson movies"
- "Play Sia music"
- "Order Domino's pizza"

And literally thousands of other requests.

To be clear, linking your Alexa enabled device like the Echo Show will allow you to control your Fire TV options on your TV. You will not be able to watch programs directly on your Echo Show screen.

Dish TV

This service appeals mostly to those that already have a Dish TV package (www.dish.com/programming/packages), which currently starts at $49.99/month plus $10/month for the Hopper DVR. Dish TV has pushed its Alexa relationship by periodically offering new customers an Amazon Echo Dot upon signup. You can check the availability of this offer at www.dish.com.

Required: Dish TV Package, DISH Hopper Smart DVR

Devices currently supported: Hopper 3 and newer, Hopper with Sling, Hopper and Wally

Benefits: Play Dish TV on Echo Show, and ask Alexa to:

- Change the channel (ex. "Go to channel 75")
- Search for shows, movies or actors (ex. "Find Modern Family on Dish" — Alexa will look for options on the services you have such as Netflix, Hulu and Amazon Prime)
- Play your recorded content (ex. "Play Dallas Cowboys football game")
- Pause, fast-forward and rewind what's being shown (ex. "Rewind 2 minutes")

Setting Up Dish TV on Alexa:

- Go to *Music, Videos & Books*
- Select *Dish TV*
- Enable the Skill
- Tip: Have your Dish TV and Amazon login information handy, since you might need to enter it during setup
- Follow the on-screen instructions to connect Alexa to Dish TV

which include 1.) turning on your Hopper setup box and TV 2.) Enter the code given on the TV screen into the Alexa App

- Tip: You might need to update your Hopper's software to the latest version before you can use Dish TV with Alexa. On your Dish set-top box, navigate to channel 9607 and locate/select "software update" to update your receiver to the latest software. Allow the software update to complete and the Hopper box to restart before returning to the Alexa app to attempt to link again

- Select *Finish Setup* in the Alexa app

- Follow on-screen prompts to link Echo Show to the TV or other equipment you use to watch TV and other video services

If you have issues with the process, try these fixes:

Update the Alexa App, and make sure you signed into the app with the same account information you used to register your Echo Show device — that is, make sure your app and device are on the same account. If not:

- Sign into the account the Echo Show device is registered with, or

- Deregister the device and reregister it on the account you typically sign in to

To deregister your Echo Show:

- Go to www.amazon.com/mycd

- Select *Your Devices*

- Select the box to the right of the appropriate device

- In the popup window, select *Deregister your device*

- Follow the onscreen prompts

Double-check to make sure you've enabled the Alexa Video Skill for Dish TV (or another video provider you're setting up)

Contact Dish TV directly

A Word about YouTube

NB At the start of October 2017 Google, the owners of YouTube, removed access to YouTube videos on the Echo Show. I have left this section, about accessing YouTube content, in this guide because I hope that Amazon and Google will come to some agreement in the near future.

Alexa and YouTube have a casual relationship at this point. There's no access to YouTube via an Alexa App page, just through voice requests. Saying, "YouTube" will get no response from Alexa, as of this writing. Saying, "YouTube Jimmy Kimmel" or "YouTube How to fix a faucet" will bring the reply, "OK, this is what I found from YouTube," and a list of recent or popular videos will be displayed. Scroll through them by sliding left and selecting the one you want to watch. The more specific your request is, the more likely you are to get the video you want. You can restrict access to YouTube using the Echo Show device Settings. S*elect Settings > Restrict Access > YouTube* where you can block YouTube search or turn on Restricted Mode.

When watching a YouTube video, it will not appear on the Alexa App player. Tap the screen for a Player with limited controls or use basic voice controls. Note that if you pause a YouTube video and don't resume it within a few minutes, it will be gone. You'll have to request it again, and no Cards are generated by YouTube videos. Because of the popularity of YouTube and the power of Google, it's possible a more integrated relationship will evolve between Alexa and the world's top video sharing sight.

5: Songs by the Millions — Music

For any voice command you read in this chapter be sure to use your wake word ("Alexa", "Amazon", etc) first.

It's difficult to beat Alexa and Echo Show for ease and convenience for playing music from a diverse range of sources.

My Music Library

This section of the app is where you access YOUR personal music collection; the next section, Amazon Music, is where you can access ALL music available from Amazon. The order seemed logically backwards to me when My Music Library was sparse, but now that I have a large Library of music, it makes sense. I access what I already have more often than I want to browse what else is available.

Your account's My Music Library will be populated with music which has been:

- Imported: These are playlists you've uploaded to your My Music account on Amazon.com from sources such as iTunes, Google Play and the Windows Media Player.
- Purchased from Amazon
- Selected in the form of a Playlist from Amazon Prime and Amazon Music Unlimited subscriptions

To import music to your music library use your pc or mac and follow these steps:

1. Go to https://music.amazon.com/home
2. Choose *"Imported"* from My Music
3. Select the blue *Upload your Music* box
4. Install the Amazon Music for PC/MAC App on your computer when prompted
5. Upload/import up to 250 songs to the Amazon cloud for free

Optional: Get an Amazon Music storage subscription for $24.99/year to import up to 250,000 songs by going to *Your Amazon Music Settings* https://amzn.to/2x8ukOX in your Amazon account, scroll down to *Music Storage* and following the instructions from there.

While we're on the topic of Amazon music subscriptions I think you'll enjoy having an Amazon Prime or Amazon Music Unlimited subscription, so here is a comparison of the two subscription options:

Amazon Prime including Amazon Music:

- Benefits: 2 million+ songs in Prime Music and a long list of shipping, shopping and media benefits that can be viewed on Amazon

- Standard annual: $99/year after 30-day free trial
- Standard monthly: $10.99/month
- Student Annual: $49 after free 6-month trial

Amazon Music Unlimited:

- Benefits: "Tens of millions of songs" according to Amazon
- Echo Plan: $3.99/month after 30-day free trial — available with any Echo device including Show

There are individual and family plans for those without an Echo device too.

For what it's worth, my recommendation is getting a Prime membership since it offers so many other benefits, and if you don't find enough of the kind of music you enjoy, consider a Music Unlimited subscription. Again you can manage all music subscriptions from this here: https://amzn.to/2x8ukOX

Let's explore the My Music Library page from top to bottom.

Whose Device: The first option, if you have more than one Echo device, is to select the device you want to play music on.

Whose Library: Select the music Library you want to access. If you have set up an Amazon Household, you can access Libraries of household members too. An Amazon Household can include up to two adults, though each must have an Amazon account, and up to four children. Creating and managing an Amazon Household is done through your Amazon account.

Here again are brief instructions and options.

1. Hover over **Accounts & Lists** near the top of the page on Amazon. com

2. Select **"Your Account"**

3. In the **"Shopping programs and rentals"** box, select **Amazon Households** to go to the Manage Your Household / Your Amazon Household Benefits page

4. Select **"Add an Adult,"** and follow the instructions including providing their login information, so they will have to give it to you or be there with you to type it in

5. And/or select **"Add a Child,"** Create and Save their Profile, and follow the link to Manage Your Content and Devices to determine the content they can access

Search your library: Use the search box to find songs or albums more quickly in your Library. As you type the search word, a list of results will begin to populate and gradually narrow the more of the term you complete. Echo Show is searching My Music Library only and will show a list very closely matching your search term or will return No Results Found if appropriate once you select Enter.

The next row is a menu of tabs: Playlists / Artists / Albums / Songs / Genres. Using them is a very straightforward process, so just a few comments will suffice for each.

Playlists: There are two sections here:

>Auto Playlists:

- **Imported** — These are playlists you've imported to Amazon Music account from your pc or mac using the instructions above

- **Purchased** — This is a list of all the songs you've purchased from Amazon, and in time it might become a very long and eclectic list.

- **Recently Added** — Just what it says — Recently imported playlists and a list of songs purchased in the last month or longer. I've been using Echo Show for four weeks, and all songs purchased in that time are in the Recently Added list.

>Prime Playlists

More than 1,700 Amazon Music Playlists have been curated, and the number is growing. When you add a Playlist from those available with an Amazon Prime subscription, it will appear here in your Prime Playlists library. Browse Playlists at <u>music.amazon.com/home</u>. Hover over a list, and a + sign will appear. Select it to add the list to your My Music library.

There are many ways to browse the Playlists on Amazon Prime and Music Unlimited. For example, on Prime, select the All Moods & Genres tab to view a drop-down menu. Scroll down the page to see Playlists that Amazon suggests for you based on your purchasing and listening history. The Top Playlists section includes trending lists, and Newly Released Playlists are just that.

https://music.amazon.com/playlists

Hover over or tap a Playlist to see your options:

- Select the + sign to add the entire list to your My Music Library "sight unseen," or later the X sign to remove it

- Choose the Play icon to listen to the list, or later, the Pause icon to pause it

- Select the three dots to:

  — Share the list: Copy the link, copy the page code to embed elsewhere, email the link or share it on Facebook or Twitter

  — Follow the list by receiving updates when it is altered, and later Unfollow

  — Open the Playlist to view how long it is, number of songs in the list, who curated the list and what its reviews are. There, you can also tailor the list by adding only the songs from it that you want as part of the list

Artists/Albums/Songs/Genres: These tabs all function the same, and you can find the music you want in two ways: Scroll down through the alphabetical list at the left or jump down to its location using the #ABCDEFG, etc., list. Of course, you can also ask Alexa to play the music you want. In my experience, it helps to be as specific as possible, such as, "Play Bruce Springsteen Born to Run from My Music Library." If I say, "Play Bruce Springsteen Born to Run," without specifying a source, Alexa will take it from My Music Library, if it's there, Amazon Music, if it's not in my library but I have Prime, and if I don't, will take it from one of my music services.

Amazon Music

For this section to be relevant, you'll need a subscription to Amazon Prime and/or Amazon Music Unlimited. Here, you can explore all Stations and Playlists available through the services you subscribe to.

Stations: It's easy to find music in tune with your preferences.

- **All Stations:** This section has two categories to browse, and when you make a selection, the Station begins to play. Popular Genres & Artists stations include Classical Focus, Top Pop, Smooth Jazz, Lullabies & Bedtime Stories and other broad categories. Each of the All Artists (A-Z) stations brings together the very best music from across the band's or artist's career. Try this feature for yourself, of course, but I rarely use it. There is no search function, and scrolling down thousands of artists is impractical. There is a scroll bar on the right, though it's difficult to see since it is black on dark gray. However, the list is so large that it is difficult to scroll slowly enough to see each entry without skipping many.

- **Genres:** This is a more reasonable way to locate music you like, but you must go two levels deep to choose stations. Search categories including Featured, Pop, Country, Classic Rock, Christian, Alternative, Reggae, Clean, World, R&B, Classical and many more. When you do, you are given the list of subgenres. For example, choosing the Classical genre gives you the choice of dozens of stations like Baroque, Classical Piano, Classical Piano, etc., and popular artists like Yo-Yo Ma, the Emerson String Quartet and Hilary Hahn.

Playlists: All available Playlists are currently categorized into four headings: Mood & Activities, Genres, Artists and Decade, and you must go to the second level to select a Playlist. Choose the category you're interested in, and then browse the Playlists available. Click or tap the one you want, and it will begin to play.

The Now Playing page will show any Station or Playlist being played, and you can use all the Player, Queue and History features discussed earlier. My one complaint is that there is no scroll bar on the app, even when viewing it on a computer, to drag up or down to speed up finding what you want.

Spotify

With 140 million users and 50 million subscribers, https://www.spotify. com is one of the largest music streaming platforms. While Spotify has a free subscription, a premium account is required for use with Echo Show. That's Spotify's choice. The current cost of a premium account is $9.99/month for those who have not tried Premium before. Besides using their service with the Echo Show, benefits include the ability to download music to your devices to listen offline, skip songs you don't like as often as you want, play any song and listen without ads. To create an account, choose an email address to link to, a password, user name and payment method, which can be a credit card or PayPal. If you choose PayPal, Spotify will connect to PayPal, and you might have to sign in. Once on PayPal, you will select which payment associated with your account you want to use.

Linking Alexa to Spotify: Once you have a premium account, select *Spotify* from the *Music, Video & Books* tab, and choose:

Link your account > Authorize the Account (If asked)

A new window will open where you will have to authorize the connection of Alexa to your Spotify account. Once you do that, return to the Alexa app where you will be asked whether you want to make Spotify your default music service. If you want to change that later, it can be done at *Settings > Music & Media > Choose default music services*. There, you can select a Default music library and a Default station service. If you want to unlink your Spotify account, for example if you no longer own the Echo Show, select Spotify on the Music & Media Music Services page, choose Spotify and Unlink Account from Alexa. On that page, you can also go to Spotify to Manage Spotify Settings such as upgrade to a Premium for Family account, view and edit your profile or see when the next Renew date is.

Using Spotify on Echo Show: If you've made Spotify your Default music service, you can use your voice or the Spotify app to play music from the service. For voice, simply request music from your favorite artist, and Alexa will play it. If it's not the Default service, you'll have to say, "Play Selena Gomez on Spotify," for example. As usual, the Player will appear on the Now Playing page and at the bottom of any other page you're viewing. Manually control Player functions using the Alexa App, with your voice – Play, Skip, Shuffle, etc., or on the Echo Show screen.

You can also control the music from the Spotify App on your mobile device or computer. If you don't have the Spotify App, select it from the Spotify page on the Alexa app. You'll be taken to Spotify to sign in using your login information. From there, choose Install App or browse music on the site. It is categorized by New Releases, what's hot on the Charts, Featured Podcasts, Your Music and additional options. A Search function is also available.

Pandora

You can use Alexa/Echo Show with a free Pandora account, which I do. If you already have an account, you can skip to *Linking Alexa to Pandora* below.

There are currently three membership levels which you can find at www.pandora.com:

- **Pandora Free:** Free; Ad-supported radio; Personalized stations
- **Pandora Plus:** $4.99/month; 30-day free trial; Ad-free Personalized stations; Better audio; Offline radio
- **Pandora Premium:** $9.99/month; 60-day free trial; Ad-free; Create new stations and playlists rather than personalizing existing stations; Better audio; No limit on skips and replays; Download music to other devices

Select the level you prefer, and you'll be taken to an account signup page. Even if you select a free trial for a paid subscription, providing an email address and password on the first page will immediately begin a free account.

Linking Alexa to Pandora: Back on the Alexa App, select Pandora from the Music, Video & Books page. Then, choose:

Link your account > Authorize the link

Using Pandora on Echo Show: Once Alexa and Pandora are linked, you'll have two options on the Pandora page on the Alexa App.

- Choose + **Create Station**, and enter an artist, genre or track to search or scroll through the **Browse Genre** section to view more than 60 genres from standards like Rock, Alternative, Classical, Hip Hop/Rap, Instrumental, Comedy and Decades to niche categories like GameDay, Mexico, Rainy Day, Pandora Local and Driving.

- Browse and choose one of the stations listed below **My Stations**, a list that will populate once you start adding stations or will be displayed immediately if you link to an existing account. Toggle Sort by date (date added) and Sort by A-Z to view the My Stations list. The first entry will always be Shuffle to mix the list randomly. There is a scroll bar on the side of the list of My Stations, but as I've said, it is difficult to see, being black on dark gray.

As usual, the Player will appear and at the bottom of the page and on the Now Playing page and can be used to control the music. Voice and Echo Show screen controls work too.

iHeartRadio

This radio network and internet radio platform offers an immense amount of content including music and podcasts provided by 800 iHeartRadio partner stations in the US, more than 1,000 artist stations and a range of other media.

There are three membership levels:

- **iHeartRadio:** No cost, but you're limited to choosing a local radio station or curated stations built around well-known artists but including similar artists.

- **iHeartRadio Plus:** $4.99/month through Alexa; Play any song on demand; Unlimited skips; Save songs to create a single playlist; Replay songs from live radio and custom stations

- **iHeartRadio All Access:** $9.99 through Alexa; Everything offered in Plus; Unlimited access to millions of songs; Listen offline on iOS and Android versions, but not yet on Alexa; Create as many playlists as you like

I tried All Access but settled on the free iHeartRadio account simply because I've got so many other music choices that I don't need a paid service. If you start out with a free account, select the Upgrade Now tab on iHeartRadio at any time to try one of the paid plans.

Linking Alexa to iHeartRadio: Select iHeartRadio from the Music, Video & Books page and then Link Your Account. Authorize the link to an existing account or create a free or upgraded account with personal and payment information.

Using iHeartRadio on Echo Show: The homepage has a search box where you can type in keywords including an artist's name, genre or city, for example. Searches return results related to your keyword, and they're divided into four categories:

- Stations — Artist Stations are titled after well-known artists to give you an idea of the flavor of the music, but each station includes songs from a range of artists. I'm currently listening to the station called Adele. The song Queue includes Rihanna, Ed Sheeran, Lorde, Ellie Goulding, OneRepublic and others in addition to Adele

- Songs — Singles by title or group name related to the keyword.

- Artists — Bands, solo acts, choirs, etc. with names related to the keyword.

- Talk Shows — Shows and podcasts with names related to the keyword.

Your second option to locate music is the Browse section with three categories to look through:

- **Live Radio:** 800+ radio stations from around the country
- **Shows:** These are mostly podcasts and the 20+ categories include

Business & Finance, Comedy, Crime, Entertainment, Politics, Spirituality and Sports. Categories contain a dozen to more than 100 show options.

- **Favorites:** You have the option to select any station or show as a Favorite, and it will be saved here for easy locating later, though it might not show up immediately.

Manually select any Station or Show, and it will begin to play. When using voice, be as specific as possible for the most accurate results.

Once playing, the content can be controlled on the Now Playing page, via the player at the bottom of any other page or with your voice. Also on the Now Playing page, you have the option to expand any selection in the Queue to:

- Tune the Station by choosing what you want to play — Top Hits, Mix or Variety. I don't know what the difference is between Mix and Variety, though perhaps seasoned iHeart enthusiasts will.
- Select the Station as a Favorite
- Rate the song with thumb up or down symbols
- Create new station around your favorite artists
- Shop Digital Music Store on Amazon for material from the artist — a new window will open to Amazon

Tunein

Tunein is one of the oldest streaming services, founded in 2002. Today, its specialties are Music, News, Sports and Talk, and Tunein carries local, national and international content. Free and Premium accounts are available:

- Tunein: Free; Stream 600+ radio stations covering the range of styles
- Tunein Premium: $9.99/month; Stream 600+ radio stations; 40,000 audio books; No ads

Linking Alexa to Tunein: On the Music, Video & Books page, select *Tunein > Link your account > Authorize the link*. You can create an account there by providing the standard information, choosing the membership level you prefer and providing payment information if you choose Premium.

Using Tunein on Echo Show: The Tunein homepage is set up much like the iHeartRadio page with a search box and more specific means of searching.

- Using the **Search Box** returns uncategorized results, unless you type in the exact name of the show or station you want, and that's a disadvantage compared with iHeartRadio. You're given a very long list of results to scroll through, and so I rarely use the function. Obviously, the more specific your search can be, the better results you'll get. You might have to try several searches using differing words or groups of words to find what you're looking for.

- The **Browse** function is more successful, and here Tunein has the edge on iHeartRadio. Select from:

  — Favorites, which is empty at first but will be populated as you "Favorite" content you like

  — Local Radio based on where you've given as your location at *Settings > Your Echo Show > Device Location > Edit*

  — Trending list of stations and shows currently popular

  — Music that is divided into 40+ subcategories for decade and musical genre

  — Talk with 30+ genre subcategories

  — Sports with 20+ subcategories including popular US, European and world sports, fantasy football and podcasts

  — News with a short list of trending shows from popular sources such as NPR, CNN and BBC, and two expandable subcategories: More Shows and Recent Episodes

  — By Location allows you to find news from continents and regions around the globe

  — By Language, with more than 90 languages offered

  — Podcasts broken into Music, Sports and Talk categories with a range of subcategories in each

Once you choose a category > subcategory from Search or Browse results, a list of shows will be displayed for you to select from. Using the App for this purpose, rather than voice, is the best method. Even if you know what you want, Alexa might have difficulty with your request if you use voice. For example, I said, "Play ESPN Outside the Lines," a popular show. Alexa replied, "Do you want me to add an outside station to your Pandora account?" No, but thanks for asking. The request, "Outside the Lines, ESPN" had Alexa take me to a random ESPN station. This again demonstrates that the more content available through Alexa, the more specific you'll need to be if using voice, and your request still might not produce the desired results. I use the app, and when I locate a station, show or podcast I want to return to, I "Favorite" it immediately, so I don't have to go searching for it later. Here's how:

- Go to the Now Playing page of the App

- If the show is at the top of the Queue, expand the options box using the down caret, select Favorite Station, and the words should light red while the Station is saved in your Favorites on the Tunein homepage, though it might not show there immediately

- If the show is in your History, then you'll have to select the show to play it and bring it to the top of the Queue where you can expand the box and select Favorite Station

SiriusXM

SiriusXM started by offering satellite radio services and has expanded into online radio where it's a good fit for Alexa and the Echo Show. There are 70+ music channels, 20+ talk and entertainment channels, 10+ sports channels, 15+ news and issues channels, traffic and weather, Latin, Comedy and more.

Alexa's relationship with SiriusXM is different than it is with iHeartRadio, Tunein, Spotify and Pandora. SiriusXM is an Alexa Skill, so the platform isn't supported to the same extent as the other services. We'll cover Alexa Skills in detail in a later chapter. It being a Skill might be why the Alexa & SiriusXM connection is more problematic. I suggest you read the information on the SiriusXM page on the Alexa App for an overview and for ratings from users. The service currently has 3/5 Stars or 60% favorable after about 1,000 ratings. Problems include connecting with and accessing SiriusXM, Alexa not recognizing login information or saying it is wrong, and linking to SiriusXM causing user's Echo and Echo Show to stop working entirely. The last issue is especially concerning, though I haven't experienced it. My experience has been that Customer Service at Sirius isn't up to speed about linking Amazon Alexa with SiriusXM at this writing.

Here's something else that might deter you from opening a new SiriusXM account, and it is due to it being a Skill rather than a fully supported service: You can't search or browse SiriusXM from the Alexa App. Using voice is the only current option. You must know the name of what you want to hear or use trial and error to find what you want. I said, "Play football on SiriusXM." The first response was, "What do you want to hear?" When I asked again, the reply was, "I couldn't find a station called 'football' on SiriusXM."

If you want to proceed and have a SiriusXM account:

- Scroll to the service's icon on the Music, Video & Books page
- Select Enable and follow the prompts. If you do not have an account and still think it's worth checking out after the caveats given, sign up for an All Access trial or paid account at https://www.siriusxm.com/amazonalexa
- Sirius will send you a confirmation email
- Select the link included to set up your password for your SiriusXM account and return to login to begin
- Then, come back to the Alexa App to select Enable and make the connection

Make sure popups are enabled in the browser or system Settings. You might have to restart your computer after enabling popups to apply the change. The SiriusXM Skill can also be Enabled on Amazon's site here: http://amzn.to/2xa89GH

6: Read or Listen...or Both — Books

For any voice command you read in this chapter be sure to use your wake word ("Alexa", "Amazon", etc) first.

Listen to and read a vast library of written material using your Echo Show and the Alexa App.

Audible

Audible is an Amazon company, and its offerings have been significantly expanded in the last few years from just audiobooks to podcasts and original content that sounds more like a radio drama than a book because it is written for voice and read by a cast. For example, the X-Files: Cold Cases audiobook is four hours of material adapted from the series and read by David Duchovny, Gillian Anderson and other original and new actors. Audible books are read in the original reader's voice, not Alexa's.

Overview: An Audible account includes:

- 30-day Free Audible trial with one free book to keep

- $14.95/month after with the option to cancel at any time

- 1 book per month, and all books chosen during your subscription are yours to keep even if you cancel

- If you don't like a book, you have an exchange period for trading it for another

- Get 30% discount on additional books

- Free Audible app that allows you to listen on all your devices

- Listen/control on Echo Show and other Echo devices with the Alexa app

- Whispersync syncing that keeps your place in an audiobook even when you switch devices
- 180,000 titles and growing daily
- Limited free titles anytime

Get Started: Here's how to get started with your Audible account

- Sign up for a free trial at https://www.audible.com/
- Sign into your Amazon account
- Choose Existing Payment Method (which will be indicated with its last 4 digits) or choose Add New Payment Method and complete its details
- Select Start Your Membership
- Select your free book
- Cancel within 30 days to avoid being charged, if desired

Connect: Once your Audible account is established, it's time to integrate Alexa/Echo Show with Audible:

- Go to the Alexa App, choose Music, Video & Books
- Select Audible from the Books section
- Select Link Account and follow the prompts
- If you already have an Audible account or have purchased Audible books in the past, the books will show up in the Audible section of the App ready to enjoy

Listen: Here's how to enjoy your Audible audiobooks on your Echo Show or mobile device:

- From the Audible section, select the title you want to hear using manual controls or voice
- It will appear on Echo Show and your Alexa App Player
- Use the available touch control options, if desired

- Say, "Read my Audible book," and Alexa will ask which book, or you can request it by title

- For books in progress, say, "Resume my Audible book"

- Use voice for controls like pause, go forward, go back, go to chapter 7, read louder and similar requests

- You can also say things like, "Stop reading in 15 minutes" and "Set a 15 minute sleep timer" to have Alexa end reading when you want

Kindle Books

Amazon's Kindle has been an innovate eBook reader since its introduction. Now you can listen to Kindle books with Alexa and Echo Show — no Kindle needed. Kindle books are read in Alexa's voice.

Overview: You can purchase Kindle books individually or choose a Kindle Unlimited. Here's what's offered:

- 30-day free Kindle Unlimited trial

- Kindle Unlimited is $9.99/month and includes unlimited reading of 1 million book titles (new and recent books are not included) and magazines

- Kindle books can also be borrowed, lent and rented. To find out more about these features visit https://amzn.to/2in5p6Q

- With an Amazon Prime membership, you can select one Kindle First early release book and borrow one additional book free each month

Get Started: Here's how to create a Kindle account

- If you love audiobooks, consider a Kindle Unlimited 30-day trial, and the books can be read on a Kindle reader or Kindle for PC

- To start a free trial, sign into your Amazon account from the Kindle Unlimited page (https://amzn.to/2vInb5Z) or Prime page on Amazon.com

- Choose Existing Payment Method (which will be indicated with its last 4 digits) or choose Add New Payment Method and complete its details

- Select Start Your Membership

- Cancel within 30 days to avoid being charged, if desired

- If you don't want Kindle Unlimited, purchase, barrow, rent or select free Kindle books

- If you already have a Kindle account, the books Alexa can read will show up in the Kindle section of the Alexa App

Connect: Here's how to integrate Alexa/Echo Show with Kindle:

- Go to the Alexa App, choose Music, Video & Books

- Select Kindle from the Books section

- You may be asked to select Link Account, and if so, follow the prompts given to establish the connection

- The Kindle books you select will appear in a list here

Listen: Here's how to enjoy your Kindle audiobooks on your Echo Show:

- From the Kindle section, select the title you want to hear or use your voice to request it hands-free

- The book will appear on Echo Show and your Alexa App Player

- Use the available touch control options, if desired, including selecting the chapter you want from the Player Queue

- Use voice for controls like pause, go forward, go back, go to chapter 7, read louder and similar requests

- You can also say things like, "Stop reading in 15 minutes" and "Set a 15 minute sleep timer" to have Alexa end reading when you want

Immersion Reading on Audible and Kindle

Selected books in the Audible and Kindle services can be listened to and read at the same time, something Amazon calls "immersion reading." Not only is the text in front of you on your phone or reader, but it is narrated and highlighted too. Amazon says this feature, "sparks an extra connection that boosts engagement, comprehension, and retention, taking you deeper into the book." Most people either love it or can't tolerate it, so if you want to give it a tree, learn more at https://www.audible.com/mt/Immersion.

7: Write it Down, Get it Done & Send a Tweet — Lists

For any voice command you read in this chapter be sure to use your wake word ("Alexa", "Amazon", etc) first.

Alexa offers convenience you'll enjoy when making a Shopping List or To-do List. Both functions are explained in detail below.

To begin, choose the Lists tab from the app Menu to see both Shopping and To-do headings. The default is to show the items on the Shopping List, but selecting the To-do List will display you its contents. Toggle back and forth to view and manage the lists.

Shopping Lists

Creating and managing a shopping list to take with you on your mobile app or to print is convenient, and you might find the process fun too, as I do. Here are your options:

Manually: Select *Shopping List* from the Lists page, type things you want to buy into the Add Item + box at the top of the page, and select the + sign or tap/hit enter

Voice: Say, "Add walnuts to the shopping list" regardless of the page showing on the Alexa App

Manage your Shopping List: Whether inputted manually or by voice, the items will appear in the list with the most recent item at the top:

• Say, "Show my shopping list," and it will appear on the screen. Then say, "Remove brown rice from my shopping list" or "Remove item number 7 from my shopping list" to take it off the list. Saying "Check off" instead of "Remove" works too. Alternately, while the list is displayed on the Show screen, swipe any item left to remove it.

- Check off a purchased or unwanted item by selecting the box to its left, and a ✔ will appear in the box, the item will be ~~crossed out~~, and the Delete option will appear on the right

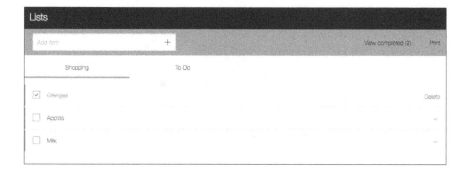

- Select the Delete option at right, if you want to remove it from the list, or leave it there as a reminder you've bought the item

- Once you go away from the list and return, checked items you haven't deleted will be moved to the **Completed** list where they can be viewed or deleted individually or all at once

- To print items, select the Active list and Print from the header

- Select the V-shaped down caret to the right for unchecked items on the Active list to:

  — Search Amazon for the item

  — Search Bing for the item

  — Move item to the To-do List

  — Delete item

Hear your Shopping List: I say, "Shopping list" to hear it because efficiency appeals to me. If you're more conversational, say "What's on my shopping list," or anything similar. The Alexa voice recognition technology has its voice-recognition "ears" open for "shopping list" almost regardless of what else you say. Try it!

View your Shopping List Active and Completed on the App: Once you create a list, leave the page and return, there are two views of it available on the App. When on your Shopping List, toggle between Active and Completed at the top of the box. The Active list is items you haven't purchased or checked off. The Completed list is items you've checked off but haven't deleted.

View your Shopping List on Echo Show: Any time you use voice to manage your list, the Shopping List will appear on the Echo Show screen for about 30 seconds.

To-do Lists

There are just a few differences when creating and managing this list compared to the Shopping List.

Manually: Select *To-do* from the Lists page, and type tasks into the Add Item + box at the top of the page

Voice: Say, "Add call the accountant to the to-do list" regardless of the page showing on the Alexa App

Manage your To-do List: Regardless of how inputted, the items will appear in the list with the most recent item at the top

- Say, "Show my to-do list," and it will appear on the screen. Then say, "Remove repair the faucet from my to-do list" or "Remove item number 5 from my to-do list." Saying "Check off" instead of "Remove" works too.

- Check off a completed task by selecting the box to its left, and a ✔ will appear in the box, the item will be crossed-out, and the Delete option will appear on the right

- Click or tap the Delete option at right if you want to remove it from the list, or leave it there as a reminder it is complete

- Once you go away from the list and return, checked items you haven't deleted will be moved to the Completed list where they can be viewed or deleted individually or all at once

- To print items, select the Active list and Print from the header

- Select the down caret to the right of items on the Active list to:

  — Move item to the Shopping List

  — Delete item

  — See what Alexa heard, so you can adjust what you say (there doesn't seem to be any voice training related to this response)

Hear your To-do List: Unfortunately, saying, "To-do list" won't deliver a reading of the list. Instead, Alexa will ask, "What can I add to your To-do list," or similar. You will have to say, "Read my," "Tell me my," or "What is on my" To-do list.

View your To-do List on Echo Show: The list is always visible on the App. To see it on the device, say "Show my To-do list" or similar.

View your To-do List Active and Completed Tasks on the App: Toggle between Active and Completed lists at the top of the box. The Active list is tasks you haven't finished. The Completed list includes tasks and projects you've checked off but haven't deleted.

As is the case when learning about any Echo Show and Alexa talent, some casual practice with creating and managing Shopping and To-do Lists should prove fun and entertaining when a dose of patience is included!

Tweet your Accomplishments

Alexa supports a feature known as IFTTT or If This, Then That. The feature is discussed later in the Help & Feedback chapter. One of the IFTTT tricks you can do is to have your Twitter account send a tweet that you've completed a task on your To-do list. Some accomplishments are worth letting the world know about! See the IFTTT section later or go to www.ifttt.com/amazon_alexa for this hack and many more.

8: Never Forget, Always Be On Time (& More) — Reminders, Alarms & Timers

For any voice command you read in this chapter be sure to use your wake word ("Alexa", "Amazon", etc) first.

Alexa and your Echo Show shine as a personal assistant in these categories. While reminders and alarms are similar, let's look at them separately to learn the nuances of each.

Home	Add Reminder	
Now Playing		
Music & Books	Remind me to...	
Lists	Fri, September 22, 2017	
Reminders & Alarms	1:45 PM	
Skills		
Smart Home	CJ's Echo	
Things to Try	Cancel	Save

Reminders

This is a quick, easy way to avoid forgetting something urgent or important. A friend of mine stops by to see her elderly father several times a week and sets Reminders for him for the following day or two. When she can't get there in person, she calls her dad and does it remotely with her father's phone on Speaker mode.

Reminders can be set and managed manually or with voice, though using voice is easier.

To set and manage Reminders manually:

- Go to the Reminders & Alarms page where tabs for Reminders, Alarms and Timers appear

- Select Reminders

- Select + Add Reminder, and a form will appear

- Fill in the spaces for Remind me to..., Date and Time

- Select which device you want the reminder to be given on

- Select Cancel or Save as appropriate

- Your reminders appear on the Reminder page in chronological order of when they will occur, not when created

- Manage any Reminder by selecting it, and you'll be taken to a page where you can Edit it or Mark as Completed

- If you select Edit, you'll be taken to a page where you can edit the Reminder by selecting any of the details or Delete the Reminder

- When editing a Reminder using the App on a computer, you must click away from the detail you edited, so that it is not highlighted, before the Save option becomes active

To set and manage Reminders with voice:

- Say "Remind me to call the mechanic at 1pm"

- If you forget to give a time, Alexa will ask for one, and if you say "1," Alexa will ask, "Is that 1:00 in the morning or afternoon?" or similar

- If you specify time but not date, Alexa will set up the reminder for today, so be sure to give the day, such as "tomorrow" or "Wednesday" for days this week, or give a date such as October 6

- When the Reminder information is given, the Reminder will display on the Echo Show screen with the two Reminders it is closest to in time, and Alexa will say, "Okay, I'll remind you at 1pm"

- To cancel a Reminder, use the day and time rather than what you wanted to be reminded of, so say, "Cancel the reminder for 1pm today," and Alexa will ask for clarification if needed

- **Note:** You cannot currently edit a Reminder using voice

To see and manage Reminders on the Device screen:

- Say, "Show my reminders" and the list will display

- To cancel a Reminder, swipe it to the left, and it will disappear from the screen and the list in the App

Getting your Reminders: With the default setting, your Echo Show displays "It's 1pm. Here's your reminder," gives a two-tone chime, and Alexa says, "Here's your reminder: Call the mechanic." The sequence happens twice a few seconds apart unless you select Dismiss on the touch screen. The Reminder will stay on the screen until you select Dismiss or take another action such as change the volume that causes the screen to display something different.

Completed Reminders: Select the Completed Reminders tab from below the active list to view them. You're not currently able to delete them from this list. They might jog your memory about whether you did something on the list, though being reminded of it is not a guarantee you followed through. For example, a completed reminder on this list doesn't mean a person remembered to take their medication or feed the dog.

Alarms

Alexa gives you a range of alarm options which we'll get to shortly, but first, here are the basics. Oddly, you currently cannot set an alarm manually, only using your voice, so let's begin there.

Setting and managing Alarms using voice:

- Say, "Set an alarm for 6am"

- Alexa will display the alarm and say, "Alarm set for 6am"

- Say "Cancel the alarm for 6am," and Alexa will say, "6am alarm canceled"

- If an alarm is on and you request another alarm for 7am, Alexa will say, "Second alarm set for 7am," and both alarms will show on the App and on the Echo Show screen

- For repeating alarms, say, "Set an alarm for":
  — 6am every day
  — 2pm every Friday
  — 7:30am on weekends

- If you forget to specify AM or PM, Alexa will ask, "Is that 6 in the morning or the evening?" and you can reply without using the wake word as long as the bar on the Show screen is green-blue to indicate Alexa is still listening

- If you don't respond, Alexa will ask again after a few seconds, and if you don't respond to the second query, no alarm will be set

- All Alarms appear on the main Alarms page with boxes turned On/ Off, indicators shown such as "Every day," with On alarms listed first

Managing Alarms manually:

- Go to **Reminders & Alarms** and select **Alarms**

- Use the box next to any alarm to turn it On and Off as desired

- Select any Alarm to edit it, and a page will display where you can edit the Time, Alarm Sound, choose Repeats options including Never and Delete the alarm if you wish

- When you've edited the alarm, select Save Changes or Cancel

Manage Alarm Volume & Sound manually:

- Select **Manage alarm volume and default sound** from the main Alarms page, and you'll be taken to a page in Settings (though here, we discuss just sounds related to Alarms)

- Change the Alarm, Timer and Notification Volume by dragging the button on the slide bar (Note that this does not change the volume for any other device function)

- Under Custom Sounds, the **Alarm** box will show the Alarm Default Sound, which can be changed by expanding the box using the > shaped caret

- From the list of **Alarm Default Sounds**, select Celebrity to see an expanded list of celebrities who have lent their voice to Alexa or scroll down Custom sounds to select one

- Sounds can also be managed on the Echo Show screen at Settings > Sounds

Timers

If you're like me, you'll eventually use Timers for a range of purposes, some which overlap with Reminders. These are simple functions, so this can be quick:

- Timers can be set for 1 second to 24 hours

- Timers must be set with voice, so say, "Set a timer for 45 minutes" or "Cancel the timer"

- Multiple timers can be set to run concurrently

- Active timers will display on the Show screen for a few seconds at the beginning or if you say, "Show me the timer"

- Active timers will display and count down on the App

- Timers are also cancelled by swiping them left when they're displayed on the device screen or by selecting them on the App and choosing Cancel

- Select Manage timer volume to be taken to the Settings page to adjust Alarm, Timer and Notification Volume

9: Let's See What She Can Do — Alexa Skills

For any voice command you read in this chapter be sure to use your wake word ("Alexa", "Amazon", etc) first.

Alexa Skills are voice-driven capabilities performed through your Echo device. There are more than 15,000 Skills, and the number grows daily. Skills are loosely grouped into 20 categories currently.

Get Familiar with Skills: Start your Skills adventure by getting to know what's available. There are three ways to browse Skills, and all begin on the Skills page on the Alexa App Menu. The default setting on this page is to show All Skills. Near the top right is a tab called Your Skills, which will be populated as you enable Skills for your use. Once you are adding Skills, you'll likely toggle back and forth between the All Skills and Your Skills lists quite a bit. OK, let's explore starting on the Skills home page in the Alexa App.

Option 1: Scan the rows of Skills labeled Top, Recommended, Trending, New, Most entertaining, etc. Each row can be scrolled horizontally using the arrow at the right to view additional Skills in the category.

Option 2: Explore the **Categories tab** which jumps you down the page to where Skills are organized in 20 categories including:

- Newest Arrivals
- Business & Finance
- Food & Drink
- Games, Trivia & Accessories
- Health & Fitness
- Movies & TV

- Music & Audio
- News
- Productivity
- Shopping

Select any category to browse the Skills in it. There will be two rows of Skills that can be browsed by sliding left or using the arrow on the right of the page:

- Recommended for You based on Skills you already have, your search history and other factors Amazon plugs into an algorithm to determine what you might like
- Top Enabled Skills based on the popularity of the skills

These rows are followed by a list of all the Skills in the category. It can be a long list! Currently, there are nearly 500 Skills in the Health & Fitness category, so rather than scrolling through the options, I used the search box to narrow the list to skills related to a personal interest such as biking. Four results appeared. If there were many results, I would use the Sort By option at the top right of the results list to narrow the search by Relevance (default), Average Rating or Release Date.

Option 3: Use the Search box to find a Skill for something very specific (e.g., ecobee, weather Canada, Corvette) or to see if there is one related to one of your interests. For a random sampling, I typed in:

- "Chinese" and received 35 search results related to learning the language or one of the dialects, cuisine, the Chinese calendar and zodiac, etc.
- "Flowers" — 17 results about ordering flowers, facts and trivia, state flowers, etc.
- "Michigan" — 89 results about trivia, history, several state universities, winning lottery numbers, snow reports for skiing, information from news outlets, etc.

The results can be narrowed using the Sort By options at the top right of the results list or by adding a word or two to your search query — Chinese language, or University of Michigan, for example. For something like "news" with more than 3,200 results, you'll have to search a specific news organization, news about a topic, city, event or similarly narrow term.

Enable Alexa Skills and Use Them

When you're ready to put a Skill into action, the first step is to enable it, which is like turning it on for use with your Alexa account and Echo devices.

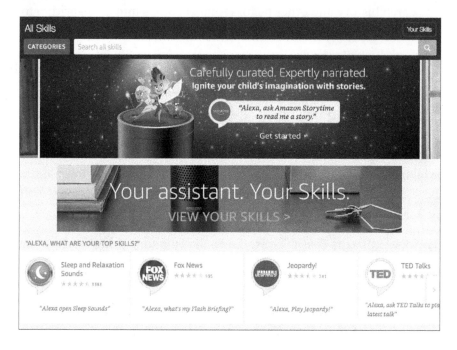

It's important to note that some of the Skills require creating and/ or linking to an account or subscription separate from Amazon, so additional steps might be required. Recently, I enabled the Allrecipes Skill and discovered I had to open an account on the Allrecipes site and link to it to get the most from the Skill.

Here's how to enable and use an Alexa Skill:

- Use one of the options above to locate a skill you want to enable, and select the skill

- Select Enable Skill, and after a few seconds, the box will switch to Disable Skill, which means it's been enabled and will appear in the Your Skills list

- Alternately, say, "Enable the Rainforest Sounds Skill"

- You can also browse and Enable Skills on Amazon.com (https://amzn.to/2iGfA6u)

- To use any Enabled Skill, include the name of the Skill and make a request such as "Play rainforest sounds"

- **Note:** Skills in use do not appear on the Now Playing page or Player, so to control them, say "Stop," "Pause," "Resume" or similar

Get the Most from the Skills You Enable

The more familiar you are with the Skill's capabilities, the more it will benefit you. Here are suggestions for optimizing a Skill's usefulness:

- If another action is offered along with Enabling the Skill, such as Manage in News Briefing (common for Skills from news organizations, and covered later), select the option to learn about it and decide whether to use the feature

- Read the About the Skill section to acquaint yourself with its capabilities

- Review the Try Saying suggestions to get the Skill to do what you want and additional suggestions in the About information

- Learn the ***Invocation Name*** for the Skill (found under Skill Details) to be sure Alexa will put it to work when you want to use it

- Browse the Customers Have Also Enabled section for similar or complementary ideas

- Read reviews, and, if interested, add a review after you've used the Skill for a few weeks

- Select Having Trouble with This Skill to get help using it from the source of the Skill

Disable an Alexa Skill

Over time, the Your Skills section can become crowded with Skills you don't use. They're easy to remove.

• Select the Skill from Your Skills list

• Select Disable Skill, and the box will flip to Enable Skill to indicate it isn't enabled and the Skill will disappear from your list

Develop an Alexa Skill and Share It with the World

As you browse Skills, you'll notice the name of the developer next to each. There are Skills from large companies like Capital One and Starbucks, but most of the 15,000+ Skills are developed by small companies, entrepreneurs and hobbyists.

Amazon has a Developers Site dedicated to creating Skills where you can go through the process: Learn/Design/Build/Launch. The Amazon Skills Kit (ASK) is an online center for developers. Build one from scratch or use templates available for several types of skills. Amazon offers rewards to developers such as Echo devices, Amazon dev shirts and Amazon Web Services (AWS) credits.

A Word about IFTTT

Those letters stand for *IF This, Then That.* An IFTTT is a shortcut, now called an Applet, that allows you to accomplish a task by completing/ saying something unrelated. A few examples are:

• When you check off a task on your To-do list, an IFTTT Applet sends a tweet through your account to let your followers know it

• When you ask Alexa what's on your Shopping List, the Applet sends you an email with your list included

• When you ask Alexa to find your phone, the IFTTT calls the phone (or when you ask Alexa for a weather forecast, the IFTTT calls your phone. The IFT and the TT don't have to be related in any way.)

Note: Alexa can't be the "Then That" part of the equation. For example, you can't have Alexa give you an email notification or order a pizza through an IFTTT.

IFTTT skills are easy to set up on the Alexa channel of the IFTTT website. Explore the Applets already produced, or create your own:

- Go to www.ifttt.com/amazon_alexa

- Sign in or create an account

- Select Connect

- You'll then be taken to a Sign in page for your Amazon account to link Alexa with IFTTT

Once you've Turned on a particular Applet you will then be able to use the appropriate voice command to carry out the action.

Just a few years ago, IFTTT hacks were trending. Now, IFTTT is hard to find, buried deep at Settings > Help & Feedback > Echo Show Productivity > More About Productivity > IFTTT. These days, there's a Skill for everything that used to be accomplished with an IFTTT. Therefore I suggest you, instead, search the Skills section of the Alexa app for the things you'd like to do, browse the results, enable a Skill and put it to use. The process is far simpler.

What I've Learned About Skills

I've explored more than 500 Skills and Enabled more than 200 in the last few months. My Skills list currently has 44 Skills; I use some daily and others only occasionally.

The Skills I rely on the most are those that save me time, are easy to use and/or offer genuine value. If they're a hassle, a time-waster or not the easiest or best way to do things, I either disable them immediately or as soon as the novelty wears off or when I occasionally go through the list to get rid of unused Skills. Some have features that are easy to use and features that are a hassle. For example, when I have a specific recipe in mind, I bring it up on the Allrecipes Skill and it's a delight to use. However, browsing recipes to get meal ideas is tedious using the Skill, so I go to the Allrecipes.com site on my computer or phone.

You'll soon see that there are sometimes several Skills for some purposes. Searching Skills for "find my phone" yielded six results, "restaurant finder" showed ten options and "control lights" produced a list of 25 smart home Skills. In the case of light control, some of the Skills require a specific brand of home automation equipment. Look for your brand's logo in the results list. If you don't find it, explore some of the top-rated Skills by reading the About information, Requirements for its use and Reviews. Reading the information is a good approach when choosing any Skill from a results list.

When I'm undecided about which of two or three Skills to choose, I enable both or all and use them alternately. I often use one right after another, and do that every day for a week or so. This is a better way to determine which Skill is right for me than to try one for a week and then try another. I like an immediate, one-after-the-other comparison.

The point I'm delicately trying to make is that there are many Skills that...just aren't very good. It's worth putting in some time to find the gems that you'll use over and over, but be prepared to wade through quite a lot of rubbish!

10: 21ˢᵗ Century Living — Smart Home

For any voice command you read in this chapter be sure to use your wake word ("Alexa", "Amazon", etc) first.

If you're already integrating smart technology into your home, then learning to control it with Alexa's help will be one of the easier parts of the curve. There's a four-step process that is straightforward and usually successful. If you're new to smart home devices then I recommend you visit the Amazon Smart Home page (amzn.to/2wHRFJW) to familiarize yourself with the possible options.

Smart home tasks are considered Skills and used as such. You'll be well-prepared for the information here if you've read the previous chapter and enabled a few Skills.

Here are the steps. Each is explained in detail below:

1. Prepare your smart home device for linking

2. Enable the Skill associated with the smart home device

3. Ask Alexa to discover the device to connect the two and to use Alexa to control the smart home device

4. Use the Alexa App to organize your smart home devices for optimal use

Amazon suggests we cover a few common-sense security tips for using smart home devices with Alexa, so let's do that first:

• Follow the device's instructions for safe, recommended uses

• Confirm that requests have been carried out — especially tasks related to your home's safety and security (security system, exterior lighting, door locks, garage door, HVAC, appliances, and similar)

- Turn off the microphones on Echo Show and other Alexa device if you do not want Alexa to respond to voice commands when safety and security cannot be ensured (such as when adults are away from home)

- Remember that once a device is connected, anyone can use Alexa/ Echo Show to control it, so make sure those in your household and guests understand safe operation of smart home devices

Okay, let's get rolling.

Step 1: Prepare your Smart Home Device

This step ensures your device is compatible and optimized for use with Alexa:

✔ Verify that your smart home device is compatible with Amazon Alexa, which can be done by searching for it on the Skills page of the Alexa App or Amazon.com, checking the packaging, contacting the manufacturer or viewing its website and looking for the device on the **Alexa smart home shopping page** that includes all compatible devices (https://amzn.to/2wITbeJ)

✔ Download the manufacturer's app for the smart home device to any device you're using to manage the Alexa app

✔ Use the manufacturer's app to set up the smart home device/ equipment on the same Wi-Fi network your Echo Show is on

✔ Download and install the latest software updates for the smart home device

Note: V1 Hue Bridge devices from Philips currently can only use Alexa for on/off and brighten functions on Echo, Dot and Tap. Functionality for Show is expected soon, perhaps by the time you're reading this. To discover your Echo devices, push the button on the Hue Bridge and say, "Discover devices."

Step 2: Enable the Device's Skill

If your smart home device is compatible with Alexa, it will have its own Skill.

✔ Locate the Skill by going to the main Smart Home page on the Alexa app and searching for it under Configure Smart Home main Skills (alternately, Skills can be search on the Skills page on the Alexa App or on Amazon.com (https://amzn.to/2iGfA6u)

✔ Select the Skill

✔ Read the About information and the Skill Details on the device page that opens to familiarize yourself with its capabilities such as viewing a smart home camera on Echo Show

✔ Select the Enable button, and when it changes to Disable, you'll know the Skill is enabled

✔ When prompted, sign into the smart home device account to link it to your Alexa account

✔ Follow any prompts given to complete setting up the smart home device on Alexa

Note: A list of your Enabled smart home devices will populate on the Smart Home main page. Select any of the Skills to Disable it or to learn more about it.

Step 3: Ask Alexa to Discover the Device

This can be done two ways:

✔ Say, "Discover devices"

✔ Go to the Smart Home page on the App, select Devices, and then select the Discover tab

Step 4: Set Up Groups and Scenes for Your Smart Home Devices

As you connect smart home devices to Alexa, you can set them up to use in the way you prefer.

✔ Chose the Groups tab on the main Smart Home page

— Choose Create Groups to connect two or more devices that will work together with a single command

— Follow any additional prompts to complete formation of the Group including naming the group and selecting devices for the group

— Try the Group by making a request of Alexa appropriate to the Group's functionality ("Turn on the lights," or "Lock the doors," for example)

— To edit the Group, select it and choose the name to change it or select/deselect devices you want in the group

— To delete a group, select Delete this group

✔ Choose the Scenes tab on the main Smart Home page

— Follow the prompts to create scenes with your connected smart home devices

— Select the scene to edit or delete it

Note on naming groups: Alexa uses voice recognition to understand what you say and connect it with digital content such as the name of a group you type into the app. For this reason, give groups names that won't confuse Alexa. "Bedroom lights" is better than "B3d00m lites," for example.

If Alexa Doesn't Discover your Smart Home Device

Try these tips in this order. They will troubleshoot and solve most issues.

Device Issues:

- Double-check that:
  - Your smart home device is compatible with Alexa
  - That you have Enabled the device's Skill
  - That you have downloaded the device's app
  - That you have downloaded the latest software updates for the device
  - For a Philips Hue Bridge, be sure to press the button on the Bridge before trying to discover devices
  - **Note:** Additional details for these steps are found in the four steps above
- Restart your Echo devices including Echo Show, and restart your smart home device
- Disable and Enable the smart home device
- In the Alexa App, choose the Forget option for the smart home device to unlink it from Alexa, and then try to reconnect it

Wi-Fi Issues: The Echo Show and your smart home devices must be on the same Wi-Fi network. Personal networks are best; school and work networks you don't control might not allow unrecognized devices to connect.

Check or change the Wi-Fi network for Echo Show by:

- Choosing Settings on the Echo Show screen by sliding from the top down

- Observing what network the Show is on beneath the Wi-Fi option

- Changing the Wi-Fi network your Echo Show is on, if necessary

- Using the Add a Network option to add a network for your Echo Show and smart home devices

Note: Some smart home devices can only connect to the 2.4 GHz Wi-Fi band. If you have a dual-band network, make sure it is set to the 2.4 GHz band.

Change confusing group names: Alexa won't comprehend words with numbers or symbols in them like kitch3n lights or #kitchen lights@, so make changes to group names, if necessary.

Discover your smart home devices again: If you've made any changes discussed here, including the Wi-Fi network or band or a group name say, "Discover devices." Alexa will let you know if they are found or will say "I didn't find any devices." If this occurs, contact the smart home device manufacturer for further assistance, since it is up to the device manufacturer, not Amazon, to ensure that their devices are compatible with Alexa devices.

11: Your Highly Capable Personal Assistant — Things to Try

For any voice command you read in this chapter be sure to use your wake word ("Alexa", "Amazon", etc) first.

This is a large section of the Alexa App and could be a book of its own. There is an abbreviated section of Things to Try on the Echo Show screen at **Settings > Things to Try**.

The good news is that many of the Things to Try have been discussed in other sections, and the ones I don't talk about anywhere are very straightforward and easy to use with the few words of explanation given in the Alexa App. Our purpose in this chapter is to shed light on Things to Try that haven't been mentioned but require some explanation.

To get started, select the **Things to Try** tab on the Alexa App to explore them for yourself or to follow along with this discussion. The Things to Try section is just a list. When you select any of them, you will usually be taken to the Help & Feedback section for an explanation. The list serves as an easy place to find topics you want more information about. Things to Try is also accessible on the screen. Slide down to show options, and tap Settings. Slide the screen up to show Things to Try. The list is not in the same order on the screen and on the App.

Here are some of the useful and interesting Things to Try that haven't been detailed already in the book:

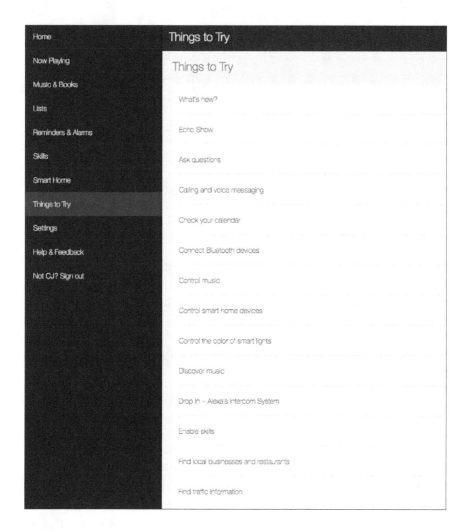

What's new?

I like to keep up with Alexa's capabilities, so I check this section weekly, at least. There's always something new. It's a mixed and disorganized bag ranging from simple, fun stuff ("Drum roll") to interesting information (the ability to give publication dates and authors for popular books) to new Skills ("Give me a quote") to new Alexa-enabled devices (this week, TV remotes from Sony, Logitech and Broadlink). It's a potpourri of fresh possibilities with Alexa and Echo Show.

Ask Questions

If you can think it, the question might be worth asking. I ask these types of questions quite often:

- What time it is here or elsewhere

- Conversions of weight, measurements temperature, money

- Spellings/synonyms/definitions

- People and place fact

- Math

Check and Manage Your Calendar

Alexa can link to calendars from Google, Apple and Microsoft

- Go to Settings, and scroll down the Account section to Calendars

- Choose the calendar you want to connect, and select Link
  _____ account

- Link another calendar, if desired

- Say, "Show me my calendar," "What's on my calendar," "What's my next appointment" or similar

- Say, "Add a 9:30am meeting to my calendar"

Discover new Alexa Skills

See the chapter (page 64) dedicated to Alexa Skills, but if you want to hear about the latest releases:

- Say, "What are popular Skills?"

- Say, "What new Skills do you have?"

- Browse the Skills store mentioned earlier where every Skill can be found and Enabled (http://amzn.to/2xOQ9pi)

Find Local Businesses and Restaurants Plus Reviews

If you haven't set your location yet, this is a good time to do that, so Alexa knows where to search. In the App Settings, select your device. In the General section of the Alexa App, select Device location and Edit, if the location is incorrect. Add as little as your zip code or as much as your full address. The more information you provide, the more accurate Alexa can be in telling you how far you are from businesses and restaurants. This task can be done on the Echo Show screen at **Settings > Device Options > Device Location**.

With Echo Show, results will be displayed on the screen, about three at a time, with the business name, a short description, its distance from your location and Yelp rating with number of reviews. To see more results, slide the screen left. Use the touch screen to select a listing for its street address, phone number and business hours, if available. Here are things to try:

- "Find a Mexican restaurant"

- "Is the post office open"

- "What clothing stores are nearby?"

- "What supermarkets are near me?"

- "What is the phone number for B&V Asian Market?"

Your search doesn't have to be local either. When planning a trip, you can ask Alex to find any of these things in another town.

- "Is there a shoe store in Grand Rapids?"

- "Pharmacy in Plano, Texas"

- "Is there Crossfit in Raleigh, North Carolina?"

All searches produce Cards, so you'll have the results right in front of you on the Alexa App. Search results might be varied, especially when there are few good options. When using Echo in a rural area, I requested a "sporting goods store," and got one accurate result and four others ranging from a used firearms dealer to a marina. See you how do with your searches!

Find Traffic Information

Alexa can give you an estimated time for your commute and the fastest route.

- In **Settings** on the Alexa App, scroll to the **Accounts** section
- Select **Traffic**
- Add or change your current address, your "From,"
- Add a destination, your "To"
- Stops along the way can be added too
- Later, select Change address to edit any of the locations

While I use this for the drive I make most often, it can be convenient for determining the time for other driving routes by changing the "From," "To" or both.

Weather Information

Once Alexa knows your location in **Settings > Your Device > Location**, you can hear or view local weather information on Echo Show and on the Card produced. Ask about weather in other cities around the globe too. Common questions Alexa can answer include:

- "What's the weather?"
- "Show me the forecast"
- "Will it rain tomorrow?"
- "How warm will it be today?"

There are many ways to answer the question, but Alexa replies to all of them with the same information — verbally sharing current and expected weather conditions for the next 24 hours and showing an extended forecast.

Go to the Movies

This section uses your location to access local movie schedules and can give you information for movie schedules in cities you'll be visiting. I get the best results with questions like these:

- "What movies are playing?"
- "What movies are playing at [name of theater complex]?"
- "When will Indiana Jones play tomorrow?"
- "Show me the trailer for the movie Dunkirk"
- "Tell me about the Aquaman movie"

Hear the News

Alexa offers something called a Flash Briefing. Many news and entertainment organizations including NPR, NBC, FOX, BBC and ESPN make brief overviews of the news, such as you might hear at the top or bottom of the hour, and those summaries can be added to your Flash Briefing.

To select which summaries you want to hear in your Briefing, and to start and manage it:

- Go to **Settings > Flash Briefing** to toggle On or Off the default options, if there are any
- Go to Skills and search your favorite news, sports, weather and entertainment stations (there are new media coming onboard every week), and enable the Skill
- If it offers a Briefing summary, that will show in your list of Flash Briefing choices in Settings
- Toggle On or Off the briefings, and you can make changes when desired
- Ask "What's the news," "Give me my flash briefing," "Flash briefing," "What's in the news?" or something similar, and you'll hear the entire briefing, one organization at a time

- If the news organization offers video with its briefing, it will play on the Echo Show screen
- The briefing does not show on the Now Playing page or the Player, but on the touch screen, your Flash Briefing can be controlled with standard control buttons

Sports: Keep Up with Your Pro and College Sports Teams & More

Give Alexa a team name and say, "score," and you'll hear the score of the most recent game. If you want to hear the latest scores and the next game for all the teams you follow, go to **Settings > Sports** to search and select those teams. Then, you'll get the answer when you ask questions like:

- "Sports scores"
- "When do the Seattle Mariners play next"
- "NBA scores"
- "Score for Real Madrid"
- "How many touchdowns did Odell Beckham junior score?"
- "How many homeruns does Aaron Judge have?"

Many major colleges can be followed too in football and basketball.

The leagues currently supported on the Alexa App are:

North American Leagues:
- MLB — Major League Baseball
- MLS — Major League Soccer
- NBA — National Basketball Association
- NCAA — National Collegiate Athletic Association
- NFL — National Football League
- NHL — National Hockey League
- WNBA — Women's National Basketball Association

European Leagues:

- English Premier League

- FA Cup — Football Association Challenge Cup

- German Bundesliga

- UEFA Champions League

Shop Amazon (for Prime Members)

Did you hear about the 6-year old girl in Texas who ordered a dollhouse with Alexa or Jimmy Kimmel's prank of telling Alexa to order pool noodles during his show broadcast into millions of US homes?

These are cautionary tales about shopping via Alexa, but with precautions, you'll be immune from such surprises.

To shop on Amazon, you'll need:

- A Prime membership (a 30-day free trial is available)

- A US shipping address

- A payment method stored with Amazon in your account's 1-Click settings

- Voice Purchasing enabled in the Alexa App at Settings > Voice Purchasing

- (Optional) A 4-digit code in Voice Purchasing that you'll have to give as a safeguard against unauthorized shopping, accidental purchases and not-so-funny pranks

- Use Manage 1-Click Settings in this section to be sure you have a payment method connected to 1-Click

- An Echo device and the Alexa App

Once you're set up, you can browse on Echo Show and order Prime-eligible items with Alexa. Here's how my shopping with Alexa usually goes when I'm not sure which product I want:

- I say, "Shop coffee makers," and then browse them on the Show screen by swiping to the left

- I select Details of any product to learn more including color options, sizes or to Add to Cart

- When I make the decision to buy, I select "Buy This," and the order is placed

- If I get buyer's regret immediately, I say, "Cancel my order, and it's cancelled"

- Canceling orders after a short time must be done online

- When the order ships, Alexa gives me a voice notification that also shows up in *Settings > Notifications*

When I know what I want, the process is much shorter:

- "Order _____," and Alexa will ask you to confirm the order or will show several options on the Echo Show screen

- "Reorder _____," and Alexa will ask for confirmation

- "Add _____ to my cart," is an option too, and you can then go online to review your cart and place the order

You can buy digital music with Alexa if you have a US billing address and payment method stored with Amazon that is issued by a US bank. Amazon.com gift cards can be used too.

Physical goods ordered can be tracked with a simple request, "Track my order."

Calling and Messaging

This Echo feature has tremendous potential and will become more useful as the universe of Echo users expands. If you know three or more people with Echo devices, this section might be worth reading now. Otherwise, it's here when Echo catches on more broadly among your friends, family members and business contacts. You can communicate with other Alexa users if you both have devices, have downloaded the Alexa App, set up this Skill and input the contact's information correctly:

- **Setting up Calling & Messaging**

— Download the latest Alexa App for iOS 9.0 or higher here: https://apple.co/2xhWycQ

— Or for Android 5.0 or higher here: https://bit.ly/2fBWcUi

— Select the Conversations icon 🔲 on the App home page, and follow the instructions to sign up for Calling & Messaging and to verify your mobile number

— Import your contacts, and those who have signed up for Calling & Messaging will appear in your contact list

— To add or edit contacts for this service, update your phone's local Address book and then open the Alexa App

— Give your contacts names you'll remember, ask Alexa to call one of them, and Alexa will dial the number associated with that name

— Calling & messaging can be used on Echo, Echo Show and Echo Dot or between non-Echo users that have the Alexa App on their phone

— If you ever wish to deregister from Calling & Messaging, contact Amazon customer service at 1.877.375.9365.

- **Using Calling & Messaging for Calls**

— Tell your Echo-using friends and family about Calling & Messaging, and encourage them to get set up and begin using the service whether they have Echo, Echo Show or Echo Dot (though obviously only Echo Show offers video calling)

— To make a call from Echo Show, say, "Call Aunt Ellen," and Alexa will begin the call

— If you prefer, say, "Turn video off," or select the Video icon on the touch screen

— To make a call from the Alexa App, select the Conversations icon 🔲 , select the New Conversation icon, select a contact and the Phone icon for an audio-only call or the camera icon for a video call

— When someone is calling you, Alexa will let you know who is calling and display the contact on the screen, a green light will appear on your Echo device

— To answer a call, say, "Answer" or select the Answer button on the Echo Show screen

— To ignore the call, say, "Ignore the call"

— To end a call, say, "Hang up" or tap the Echo Show screen and select the end-call button

— **There's a video about calling with Alexa here:** https://amzn.to/2vJrgXz

- **Using Calling & Messaging for Messages**

— Messages are recorded and played back to the recipient rather than transcribed and read by Alexa

— To send a message from Echo Show, say, "Send a message to Sara Smith," and Alexa will prompt you for the message and send your message when you complete it

— To send a message from the Alexa App, select the Conversations icon , select the New Conversation icon, and select a contact before following the prompts, or you can select the Keyboard icon and type a message before hitting the Send button

— To reply to a message from the App, select the conversation from those shown, and press the Microphone icon while speaking your message, releasing it when done to send the message or sliding left to cancel the message

— To hear messages on the Echo Show, say, "Play my messages," when Echo Show's light bar is yellow to notify you one or more messages is waiting

— When more than one phone number is synced with Alexa, you can name the numbers and say, "Play messages for _____" to hear only your messages

— To review messages on the App, choose the Notifications icon or go to Conversations to view those with a New Notification icon, and then choose between hearing the messages and reading a transcription of them

— **There's a video about messaging with Alexa here:** https://amzn.to/2wSzRfk

- **Drop in**

  — Drop in is typically set up among devices in a single household, between family members and BFFs

  — Drop in means that people in separate parts of the home or in different homes can communicate immediately without making a formal call, or it allows you to see what's going on in the nursery when two Echo Shows are connected

  — Drop in must be enabled in the mobile Alexa App for all devices that will use the capability

  — In the Conversations section of the mobile app, select a contact and turn On the Drop-in button if they have drop-in privileges with you

  — Permission can be granted with Echo Show by saying "Show my contacts" and using the touch screen to select the contact and toggle on the drop in option, which can be turned off just as easily

  — To drop in on one of your own devices, say something like, "Drop in on my living room Echo Show"

  — The names of the devices in your home can be changed in the Settings on the Alexa App or on the Echo Show screen by selecting the device you want to rename, scrolling to Device Name and selecting Edit

  — **There's a video with complete Drop in details here:** https://amzn.to/2vJs26V

While we've covered the essential details, there is a section on Alexa Calling and Messaging FAQs located here: https://amzn.to/2xy8nJ1

12: Alexa & Echo Show: Your Perfect Fit — Settings

For any voice command you read in this chapter be sure to use your wake word ("Alexa", "Amazon", etc) first.

The Settings section is where you control how the Alexa App and Echo Show function to suit your style. Let's walk through the Settings to get familiar with their contents and how you can tailor your Echo Show's performance. Select **Settings** on the App Menu to be taken to the **Settings Main Page** where we'll get started. The Echo Show device has an abbreviated list of settings.

Devices

The first thing you'll see is a list of the Alexa enabled devices that you own and linked to your Alexa account. The word "Online" appears beneath any device when it is connected to a Wi-Fi network.

Start by selecting your device from the list, and you'll be taken to a page for basic setup, organization and information:

So these are the settings for your particular device:

Do Not Disturb: This feature keeps Echo Show quiet including preventing incoming Calls, Messages and Drop-ins.

- On the Alexa App or on the Echo Show screen at ***Settings > Do Not Disturb***, turn Do Not Disturb On, and your Echo Show's screen will be dark except for a half-moon and the time of day

- Notifications, which are discussed soon, won't be announced during this time

- Swipe the screen to bring it back momentarily to check notifications

- Toggle the button Off to end Do Not Disturb

- If the Show's light bar is yellow, notifications have arrived while Do Not Disturb was on, so say "What are my notifications," and they'll be read to you, or you can see them in ***Settings > Notifications***

At any time, say, "Do not disturb," Alexa will say, "I won't disturb you," or similar, and the screen will darken until you use the wake word again. Saying, "Turn off your screen" works too. Using the Echo Show screen, slide down to show your options, and tap Do Not Disturb.

Scheduled Off: Do Not Disturb is programmable using this feature. Here's how:

- On the Alexa App, select the Scheduled box to open Scheduled Do Not Disturb

- Once you've used this Setting, the time set for Do Not Disturb to Start and End will appear

- Toggle On the Scheduled button, and if you want to change the times listed, choose Edit at the bottom to Change/Save new times or Cancel to keep them as is

- On the Echo Show at Settings, tap the oval button to turn on Do

Not Disturb if you want it on full-time, or tap the Scheduled box to turn it on and the Starts and Ends boxes to set the times

Sounds: This is where you customize what sounds your Echo Show makes, when it makes them and how loud they are.

- **Alarm, Timer and Notification Volume:** Slide the bar left for lower and right for higher, and Echo Show will give a tone at the new volume for you to evaluate

- **Audio:** The explanation of notifications is just around the corner. This allows you to determine whether a tone is given when a notification hits your Notification List. I keep Audio toggled Off unless I'm eagerly awaiting a Notification about a package being sent out for delivery or a message returned (See Calling & Messaging).

- **Custom Sounds/Alarm:** This section was covered earlier in Reminders & Alarms, but in brief, you can select from celebrity-delivered alarm messages and custom sounds. The Default alarm shows initially; If you change it, the new choice is shown in the box.

Device Name: Once you name your Echo Show and other Echo devices on your account, the name will appear on the Settings home page and here:

- Select Edit
- Change the Name
- Select Save

Device Location: I've included my complete address to get the best information about distances to restaurants and businesses near me. You don't have to enter any location, or you can input just a street and/or zip code:

- Select the Edit button
- Input or change address information
- Choose Save or Cancel

Device Time Zone: To show the correct time on your Echo Show:

- Select a Region or United States from the top box to see your time zone options

- Select the time zone you want from the lower box

- This task can be done on the Echo Show screen at *Settings > Device Options > Time Zone*

Wake Word: The default wake word is Alexa, but you can change it to Computer, Amazon or Echo. I've tried them all, and Echo is the only viable alternative for me since I often use Amazon and Computer in conversation unrelated to Alexa/Echo Show. Doing that creates a false "waking" of the device. If you want to change the wake word:

- In the Alexa App go to *Settings > Your Echo Show > Wake Word*

- Expand the Names box with the down caret

- Select the name you want

- Save it, and you'll be taken to the previous page where the Wake Word will appear

- This task can be done on the Echo Show screen at *Settings > Device Options > Wake Word*

Measurement Units: If you prefer metric units for temperature and distance, toggle the buttons to On, which can also be done on the Echo Show screen at *Settings > Device Options > Temperature/*

Distance (separate options).

Device is registered to: CAUTION! Once you set up your Echo Show, as explained in an earlier section, your name will appear here. The note of caution relates to the option to the right Reset to Factory Defaults. This will deregister your Echo Show, and I'm aware of only two times to do this:

- If you sell or give away the device

- If you cannot get it to function properly in the future, Amazon recommends deregistering and reregistering it as a last resort

Deregistering your device can also be done online, for example if you sell your Echo Show but forget to deregister it first. To deregister any Echo device:

- Go to www.amazon.com/mycd

- Select Your Devices

- Select the box to the rleft of the appropriate device

- In the popup window, select Deregister your device

- Follow the onscreen prompts

- You can reset the device on the Echo Show screen at *Settings > Device Options > Reset to Factory Defaults*

Accounts

Once you've finished with the device settings above click back to the main Settings page. Below **Devices** you will find **Accounts**. This section gets its name because some of the Settings in it require creating and linking to a third-party account such as Pandora.

Notifications: You might be familiar with Notifications because you get them on your phone, your computer and social media. Alexa uses Notifications in Shopping, Messaging and a few other features:

- Select from this list the type you want to receive and turn the box On or Off as desired

Music & Media: This section lists the accounts you've linked to Alexa, along with the user ID for the account, and those available to use with Alexa that don't require an account. If you haven't opened an account for these services or haven't yet linked your existing account to the Alexa App, you can do those by selecting any of the music services from the Music, Video & Books tab on the App menu. Complete instructions are given in Chapter 5 (page 38). Select any of the Music Services to:

* Unlink the account if you don't use the service or Echo Show any longer

* Manage your account Settings by logging into your account on the service's site

* Manage service-specific Settings such as Enabling Custom Stations on iHeartRadio

* Learn tips for using the music service

Select the ***Choose Default Music Service*** option to choose a default music library and music station. For example, my libraries are Amazon Music and Spotify, and Amazon is my default. When I say, "Play Blake Shelton," Alexa plays music available on Amazon. If I want the music I have in my Spotify collection, I request it — "Play Blake Shelton from Spotify."

Flash Briefing: Most news services create short news summaries hourly or several times per day, in many cases to play on radio. Many of those summaries are available for playing on you Echo Show whenever you want to hear them. Most are Skills, and we've discussed Skills at length. Together, those summaries you choose make your Flash Briefing. To create yours:

* Select ***Get More Flash Briefing Content***

* Browse the list, and select the ones you want

* Enable the Skill

* Those you choose will be listed here

* Toggle on those you want to play

- Choose Edit Order to rearrange the order they are played

- Say, "Play my Flash Briefing," "What's in the news" or similar, and Echo Show will deliver it

- Each news service's logo will appear on the Echo Show screen; Some services include video

- Say, "Skip" or "Next," and Alexa will move on to the next service in the briefing

- I have 11 services in my briefing, but I often hear the top story from a service and then skip to the next or skip the service altogether.

Sports Update: This feature was covered in the Things to Try chapter (page 83), but here's a summary. The feature allows you to follow professional teams and leagues from North America and Europe plus the football and basketball teams for most major colleges in the US:

- Use the Search your Teams box to find teams you want to follow

- Click on those teams from the search results

- They will appear in your list

- Remove them by selecting the X

- Say, "Sports update" to hear latest scores and upcoming games for the teams in your list that are currently in season

- Information will show on the Echo Show screen too

Traffic: Also covered in Things to Try, your Traffic feature gives you commute times. Input a "From" location, "To" location and stops in between, if desired. Edit them to change your route, and then ask, "What's my commute."

Calendars: Alexa can link to calendars from Google, Microsoft and Apple iCloud. Link your calendars, and add items to them with basic requests such as, "Add appointment at 3pm Thursday to my calendar" and hundreds of similar things. See Check and manage your calendar in this guide's Things to Try section.

Lists: Alexa manages a Shopping List and To-do List for you in the

App. You can also link your lists on Alexa to several 3rd party list apps like AnyList and Todoist:

- Create a free basic or paid premium account on one or more of those sites

- Select **Settings > Lists**

- Choose a service and select **Link Account** to connect the account to Alexa

- Sign into your Amazon account and the list service account

- Go to the separate app of the chosen service on your phone and tap "Connect with Amazon Echo"

- Sign in

- You will then see your Alexa App To-do list on your other list service, though not with all the functionality you enjoy on Alexa and Echo Show.

If you already have an account with one of those services, connecting it with Alexa might make sense. If you don't, it's redundant if you have the Alexa App on your phone.

Voice Training: Alexa's voice recognition technology is impressive. However, if you find that Alexa misunderstands you when you make requests you know it should comprehend – "Will it rain today?", "How many cups in a quart?", "What is the capital of Wyoming?", etc., then Voice Training might be helpful. At **Settings > Voice Training**, select **Next** to start your session. The 25 phrases you'll be asked to read include the most common syllables used in English and give Alexa the opportunity to "learn" the way you say them. A sampling of the phrases includes Alexa:

- Put 'pay rent' on my to-do list

- Wikipedia, Frank Sinatra

- What's the extended forecast for Albuquerque?

Alexa fulfills the requests made in each phrase, so you can say, "Stop," if you aren't interested in learning more about Ol' Blue Eyes or the weather in New Mexico. You'll also have to undo a handful of fulfilled requests, unless you want walnuts on your shopping list and an alarm set for 6:15AM tomorrow. Each time you choose Voice Training, the request list is in a different order, so you don't have to go through the entire list, you can return and likely get new requests to repeat.

Voice Purchasing: The details on this topic are covered at length in Things to Try (page 84) under "Shop Amazon (For Prime Members)". In short, Amazon Prime members with a US address and means of payment stored on Amazon can:

- Enable 1-click shopping on your Amazon account
- Enable Voice Purchasing here
- Choose a 4-digit code and require its use with Voice Purchasing
- Order and reorder Amazon Prime-qualified items with hands-free ease

Amazon Households: When you create an Amazon Household, you gain four advantages:

- Members share Amazon Prime benefits when Prime Sharing is enabled
- All digital content can be shared between adults in the household in what Amazon calls a Family Library
- Select titles can be shared and unshared with children too
- Payment instruments/methods can be shared with other adults in the Household

A household can include up to two adults and four children. As we noted earlier, creating and managing an Amazon Household is done through your Amazon account.

On Amazon.com:

1. Hover over **Accounts & Lists** near the top of the page
2. Select "Your Account"
3. In the "Shopping programs and rentals" box, select **Amazon**

Households to go to the Manage Your Household / Your Amazon Household Benefits page

4. Enable Prime Sharing, if desired

5. Select "Add an Adult," and follow the instructions including providing their login information, so they will have to give it to you or be there with you to type it in

6. And/or select "Add a Child," Create and Save their Profile, and follow the link to Manage Your Content and Devices to manage the content they can access

7. Adults and children can be removed just as easily, and you can "leave" a household too

Leaving and removing can be done in this section of the App too. Select yourself, and choose Leave; select another Household member, and choose Remove.

Complete information about households and how to manage yours can be found on this page.

https://www.amazon.com/myh/manage

General

There are two final Settings sections, History and About the Amazon Alexa App.

History: Select this Setting to view your entire voice-interaction history with Alexa. Choose any line to see complete details or to delete the item. To delete all voice recordings and their associated Cards:

• Go to www.amazon.com/mycd

• Select Your Devices

• Select the box to the left of the appropriate device

• In the popup window, select Manage voice recordings, and Delete or Cancel

You can also deregister your Echo device or change its name there.

13: Resources Galore — Help & Feedback

This section of the Alexa App provides a wealth of information, though we've already covered much of it and referred to it frequently. When selecting an item from Things to Try, for example, you are usually taken here for the explanation. There are things worth mentioning about this section that haven't been covered yet in this guide. Note there is a limited Help section on the Echo Show at **Settings > Help**

Alexa and Alexa Device FAQs

These FAQs are difficult to find by navigating through the Help & Feedback section. You can access them on every Card though. Select Learn More in the "Remove Card" box on each Card. They are also found here:

https://amzn.to/2xy8nJ1

Let's scroll through Help & Feedback for important areas not yet discussed.

Alexa User Guide

Alexa is the cloud-based AI "brain" for all Echo devices. The Alexa User Guide includes these notable new topics:

Alexa Device Support: Sections of special interest here are:

- **Accessibility Features for Alexa** is an overview of the technology required to make Echo Show easier to view, hear and communicate with.

- **Differences Between Alexa Devices** is a good source of information if you're interested in adding other devices to your Echo-sphere

- **Supported Alexa Features** is a companion to the previous section as it lists what main Alexa features are supported by the various devices – which have Bluetooth, Calling & Messaging, alarms & timers, Flash Briefing, Music, Audible, Kindle, etc.

- **Using Multiple Alexa Devices** is must-reading if you do grow your Echo-sphere. There's information about using devices with the same Wake Word, which devices don't require a Wake Word (Amazon Tap, e.g.) and things you can do (like share Music between devices) and things you can't do (like play the same music on more than one device).

- We discussed voice-control of Fire TV in its section in the Video chapter, but the **Use Your Alexa Device to Control Your Fire TV** section in the App offers more detail and will be useful for Fire TV users for linking and controlling content.

- The **Personalize Your Alexa Device** section has all been covered, but this is a handy overview of your options. If you get a free hour, pour a favorite beverage and go through the list to customize what you want Alexa to do for you, something I do about once a month.

- **Differences Between Alexa Voice Remote for Echo and for Fire TV** is a good reminder that the capabilities of these two remotes do not overlap where it counts: The Alexa remote for Echo devices like Echo Show does not control Fire TV; the Alexa remote for Fire TV doesn't control Echo devices.

Alexa Calling and Messaging: Here is your resource for Calling, Messaging and Drop In capabilities. The information in this section and its links are comprehensive. You'll find step-by-step instructions to follow for setup and use, if what we discussed earlier isn't clear.

Alexa Quick Fixes is another section you might find useful. While we've tried to be thorough, and there's nothing new here currently, this section includes information that might have been updated since the publication of this book.

Echo Show User Guides

Most of the information in the various Echo Show User Guides has been covered, but a few sections cover fresh territory. The following list of sections shows Which Echo Show Guide the Section is in > The name of the Section

Echo Show Accessibility > Using Accessibility Features on Echo Show

This helpful section is designed for those with visual and/or hearing impairments, but anyone might find them helpful. These sections of the Alexa App explain accessibility well, and patient reading of them will clarify how the capabilities can be used.

This page is an overview of the Echo Show Accessibility Features for Vision (top) and Hearing (bottom) and a Description for each. The following three sections of the Echo Show Accessibility Guide cover key Accessibility Features in detail.

Echo Show Accessibility > Guide to VoiceView Screen Reader on Echo Show

The VoiceView screen reader allows you to navigate the touch screen with verbal help from Alexa. When this mode is on, Alexa will tell you (read to you) what you're touching on the screen. It works like this for every VoiceView Setting:

- Touch the screen to hear what you're selecting

- If that's what you want, tap the screen twice

- If it's not what you want, try again, and tap twice when you hear that you've selected what you want

To use VoiceView:

- Say, "Settings," or swipe down from the top of the screen and select Settings

- Scroll down to Accessibility, and select it

- Tap the toggle switch on VoiceView to Enable the feature

Now, you've got three more adjustments, if desired:

- **Reading Speed:** How fast do you want Alexa to read what you're touching? The range is from .66 (.66x) of normal to 4 times normal (4x). I settled on 1.25. It's slightly faster than Alexa usually speaks, but not so fast its annoying or hard to understand. **Note:** You might find it difficult to scroll up to speeds lower than Normal. Persistently swipe up on the right edge of the screen, and the slower speed options should come into view.

- **Speech Volume:** How loud do you want Alexa to read what you're touching on the screen? This doesn't affect anything else communicated by Alexa in response to a request you make. Try several volumes to find one that is comfortable. When Reading Speed faster than normal and Volume is higher, I feel like I'm being shouted at.

- **Sounds Volume:** This Setting functions like Speech Volume but for the sounds Echo Show and VoiceView make.

That's not code Alexa is talking. When you tap any of the options on this screen, Alexa will read the option to you, tell you which option you've tapped and how many are available. You will also hear whether the checkbox is checked. The first few times I tried one of these Settings, I couldn't figure out what Alexa was talking about. For example:

"Reading speed 1.5x, 5 of 10, checkbox not checked." This means you've tapped the 1.5 times normal option and that 1.5x is the 5th fastest of 10 options."

Those are the basics; the remainder of the guide is filled with useful details for fine-tuning your use of VoiceView screen reader including options for color correction. Remember that when the accessory barrier involves speech, the Alexa App can be used for most Echo Show functions, adding items to the Shopping List and To-do List and much more.

Echo Show Accessibility > Guide to Screen Magnifier on

Echo Show

If you want to enlarge what is displayed on Echo Show, this is where to enable the feature.

To use Screen Magnifier:

- Say, "Settings," or swipe down from the top of the screen and select Settings
- Scroll down to Accessibility, and select it
- Tap the toggle switch on Screen Magnifier to turn on the feature

Using Screen Magnifier is easier than using VoiceView. Once it is on, your options are to:

- Tap the screen 3 times to magnify and 3 times to return to normal size
- Once Magnifier is on, use two fingers slightly apart to pan left/right/up/down/diagonal
- Zoom in by separating your fingers, touching the screen, and pulling them together
- Zoom out by putting two fingers together, touching the screen, and separating them
- For quick-zoom, tap the screen 3 times, but leave your finger on the screen until magnification occurs. Leave your finger there, move it around to pan, and remove it to end Magnifier

Echo Show Accessibility > Used Closed Captions on Echo Show

Closed captioning will show closed captions for video when it is available. To use Closed Captioning:

- Say, "Settings," or swipe down from the top of the screen and select Settings
- Scroll down to Accessibility, and select it
- Tap the toggle switch on Closed Captioning to turn on the feature

The captioning is appropriate for the size of the Echo Show screen, which is to say it is small, but it doesn't interfere. The Closed Captions user guide gives clear direction for customizing your experience including changing the size, color and opacity of the text, the font, font edge style and more. Many of these adjustments can be explored and made on the screen at Settings > Accessibility > Closed Captioning Preferences.

Note: Some Accessibility functions can be managed on the Echo Show device at ***Settings > Accessibility***.

Getting Started with Echo Show > Navigate your Echo Show

There's nothing remarkable here, but since the Echo Show sports a touch screen, you should know your way around it including these two important capabilities:

- **Watch Amazon Video on Echo Show:** You can search your Amazon Video Library and watch movies and TV shows on Echo Show using voice and touch. While the 7-inch doesn't compare to your HDTV or 17-inch laptop screen, there might be times you enjoy viewing video on Echo Show. Having an Amazon Prime account, which includes Prime Video, will be an asset.

- To find what you'd like to watch, make requests using keywords for what you want to locate such as:
  — "Show my video library"
  — "Watch The Good, the Bad, and the Ugly"
  — "Show me Kevin Hart movies"
  — "Show me World War Two movies"
  — "Show me free movies"
  — "Show me cartoons"

Alexa often locates several options and says, "Here's what I found." Use touch to slide the list left to browse it and to select what you want to watch. If what you want to watch isn't free, you'll be asked to first rent it, buy it or subscribe to a movie service first. Selectable paid options are often shown on the screen.

Once a movie is playing, you can control it using verbal requests like "Stop," "Pause," "Play," "Go back 15 minutes," and "Put a sleep timer on for 30 minutes." Use the touch screen to play, pause, go back or forward 10 seconds.

- **View Photos You've Loaded to Amazon on Echo Show:** Amazon Prime includes Amazon Photos, a service that offers unlimited photo storage for you and five other people, whether family or friends, to form a Family Photo Vault. If you're a Prime member, you can learn more by selecting Your Prime Photos from your Account Lists. If you're not an Amazon Prime Member, a 30-day free trial for the $99/year service can be started from nearly any page of Amazon.com.

  — Go to the main Amazon Photos page: https://amzn.to/2vJg8dd

  — Once you've added photos to your prime account, view them on Echo Show using the types of commands you'd expect: "Show my photos" or "See my photo vault." Alexa will dialogue with you, and some navigation can be done using the touch screen too.

Echo Show Photos > About Photo Booth

This is a good time to mention Amazon Drive, Amazon's cloud storage service. Did you know you have an Amazon Drive account, if you have a regular Amazon account? You do. To see yours, go to ***Amazon.com > Accounts and Lists > Your Amazon Drive***.

There are four account options:

- 5 GB Amazon Digital Storage Plan – files, photos, videos and more: **Free** with an Amazon account

- Prime Photos – Unlimited photo storage plus 5 GB of storage for other files: **Free** with Amazon Prime

- 100 GB Amazon Digital Storage Plan – All types of files, and photos don't count against the 100 GB for Prime members: **$11.99/year**

• 1 TB+ Amazon Digital Storage plans – Like the 100 GB plan but much larger: $59.99/year

Price might change at any time, of course.

Now to Echo Show Photo Booth. This fun feature allows you to take Single-shot photos, 4-shot sequences and Sticker-mode shots that include fun overlays in the picture.

Echo Show Photos > Use Photo Booth

Here's where the fun begins. Take photos hands-free with the Echo Show:

• Say, "Take a photo," Alexa will ask you to pick a camera from the single-shot, sticker and 4-shot options that appear. You'll have to touch the screen and slide to the left to get to the 4-shot camera.

• Specify a camera by saying, "Take a single shot," "Take a sticker shot" or "Take a 4-shot photo"

• While Alexa is still in camera mode, make further requests, if desired

If you select Sticker Mode, you'll also need to slide left on the screen to see all options. With practice, you'll be able to frame yourself or your subject with the augmented reality "props." Once you settle on a camera and/or sticker option, Echo Show will count down to the snap of the photo, there will be a brief flash, and if Echo Show isn't muted, a camera sound. Four-shot photos are taken about one second apart, each with its own flash. Photos taken with Echo Show automatically upload to your Amazon Drive account or to Prime Photo, which can be accessed on the Amazon Drive main page.

Echo Show Photos > View Photos on Echo Show

There's a list of handy, straightforward phrases here that will direct Echo Show to display your photos to enjoy and organize them.

Contact Us

I've had no issues with Echo or Echo Show that I couldn't solve using the abundance of information found in the Alexa App and on Amazon. com. Because of the good fortune I've had with Alexa and Echo, I haven't emailed or called Customer Service. However, if you have problems and can't find answers, don't hesitate to contact Amazon. Feedback is another issue. I have used the Send Feedback option seven times to date to give Amazon my thoughts on how to improve Alexa/Echo Show performance. I bring this up to say that Amazon has always been responsive, so if you contact the company with issues, you can expect that a customer service representative will be in touch.

Legal

If you have questions about how Amazon will use your information or what legal parameters there are for using Alexa/Echo Show, scanning the Legal & Compliance section will provide you with answers.

14: Going to the Source — Amazon Pages to Be Familiar With

My goal is to provide you with clear, concise information from the perspective of someone that uses Echo Show and Alexa every day, insight I don't often find when reading pages on Amazon. That's why I wrote this book. Still, there are pages on the website that might help you get the most from your Echo device.

Alexa Help: This is a home page with links to information on the broad categories of things Alexa can provide — Music & Entertainment, News & Information, Questions & Answers and everything else covered in this book. http://amzn.to/2k5tsrI

Echo Show Help: This page, and its many links, overlaps with the Alexa Help page, but the emphasis is on Echo Show. http://amzn.to/2wZ21pH

Echo Show Videos: This page provides general overview videos for many key setup and use tasks. http://amzn.to/2wWU6cl

Before You Go

So there you have it! I trust by now you have your Echo Show up and running and have become familiar with many of its features. Please drop me a line at cjandersentech@gmail.com if you require any further clarification. And don't forget to sign up for my monthly newsletter; I will keep you up to date with the ever changing features of Alexa.

Get your updates here: https://about.me/cjandersen

CPSIA information can be obtained
at www.ICGtesting.com
Printed in the USA
LVHW04s2145061018
592678LV00003B/3/P

9 781978 440265